Using Your Home Computer

Macmillan Microcomputer Books

General Editor: Ian Birnbaum

Advanced Graphics with the BBC Model B Microcomputer
   Ian O. Angell and Brian J. Jones
Assembly Language Programming for the BBC Microcomputer
   Ian Birnbaum
Using Your Home Computer
   Garth W. P. Davies

Also from Macmillan

Advanced Graphics with the Sinclair ZX Spectrum
   Ian O. Angell and Brian J. Jones
Advanced Programming for the 16 K ZX81   Mike Costello
Beginning BASIC   Peter Gosling
Continuing BASIC   Peter Gosling
Practical BASIC Programming   Peter Gosling
Program Your Microcomputer in BASIC   Peter Gosling
Codes for Computers and Microprocessors   P. Gosling and Q. Laarhoven
Microprocessors and Microcomputers – their use and programming
   Eric Huggins
The Sinclair ZX81 – Programming for Real Applications
   Randle Hurley
More Real Applications for the ZX81 and ZX Spectrum   Randle Hurley
Z80 Assembly Language Programming for Students   Roger Hutty
Digital Techniques   Noel Morris
Microprocessor and Microcomputer Technology   Noel Morris
The Alien, Numbereater, and Other Programs for Personal Computers – with
   notes on how they were written   John Race
Understanding Microprocessors   B. S. Walker
Assembly Language Assembled – for the Sinclair ZX81   Anthony Woods

Using Your Home Computer (Practical Projects for the Micro Owner)

Garth W.P. Davies

MACMILLAN PRESS
LONDON

Published by
THE MACMILLAN PRESS LTD
London and Basingstoke
Companies and representatives
throughout the world

Typeset by RDL Artset Ltd, Sutton, Surrey

Printed and bound in Great Britain at
The Camelot Press Ltd, Southampton

British Library Cataloguing in Publication Data

Davies, Garth W. P.
    Using your home computer.
    1. Microcomputers
    I. Title
    001.64'04   QA76.5

ISBN 0-333-35217-3

Contents

Acknowledgements   *vii*

1. **Introduction**   1

2. **Computer Systems in the Home**   3

3. **The Key Steps**   10

4. **Some Sample Systems**   16

5. **Design Factors**   26

6. **More Sample Systems**   42

7. **Useful Techniques and Methods**   64

8. **The Pitfalls and the Fun**   75

Index   *81*

Acknowledgements

The author would like to express his gratitude to the following persons, without whom this book would not have come into being: Pamela Stewart, for all her work in deciphering the handwriting and in typing the entire manuscript in its several versions; Christiane Scott for her invaluable help in preparing the illustrations; Peter Gosling and Ian Birnbaum for their very helpful comments on the various drafts; my sons, Rolf and Mark, and my wife, Ellen, for being enthusiastic users of a home computer — which led to this book!

1 Introduction

I love playing with my home computer. Just playing. There lies the whole
reason for writing this book. I have enthusiastically demonstrated the wonders
of my machine and have been shown those of countless others — yet have
repeatedly found it difficult to answer the simple, but very fair, question:

'But what do you use it for?'

Oh, I have shown that it can calculate standard deviations in a flash, play chess
like a grand master, display fiendishly constructed graphics pictures, but . . .
well . . . *use* it?

It was not difficult to come to the conclusion that I was not really using this
super-clever device in any normal business sense of usefulness. Asking around, I
found that the vast majority of fellow home-computer users were proud to show
me a wide range of games, fancy demonstrations of the machine's powers,
mathematical applications and so on, but relatively few had put their machines
to what I would call real practical use.

The reason for this is, I believe, quite simple. The early users of home computers were data-processing specialists. These people were enormously interested
in the development of the microcomputer and naturally tended to write computer
programs to test and demonstrate the capabilities of this new tool. In parallel, pre-
programmed electronic games were on the market and there was great interest
generally in this new dimension in playing games. Newcomers to computing, pur-
chasing home computers in larger and larger numbers, naturally do not have the
necessary skills to create even cleverer programs, nor — much more importantly —
the essential background of *systems development*. And that is where this book
comes in.

The purpose of this book is to help anyone who owns a home computer to
use it in simple practical ways in his or her private life. So you will not find any
computer programs here, but rather ideas on how to make your computer work
for you. Someone will of course have to do the programming and I expect that
by now you have learned sufficient BASIC for this, but the point is: programming
comes *after* the ideas and processes described in this book have been looked at.

In the words of computer specialists, the normal sequence of events is a
feasibility study (to see if your idea is practical and worthwhile), followed by a
detailed 'systems analysis and design' phase — only then can the programming be
started, and on the basis of exact specifications of what is to be done.

Now fortunately one is not usually under the same constraints when using a home computer (except for money!) as would be the case in a business environment, where tight schedules have to be kept and many other people have to be involved, etc. So the rigorous procedures of business do not have to be applied in the home. However, the vast body of experience gained by now from the use of computers in the business environment is nevertheless relevant. Following certain basic steps has been proven to be invaluable in developing a computer system and this book tries to identify those, as well as pointing out the pitfalls.

Equally important, however, are the actual suggestions for putting your home computer to practical use. There are some 24 detailed ideas for these in this book, presented in a way that, it is hoped, will enable you to browse through them and select those for likely application in your environment. Hopefully, this combination of using a simple but systematic approach together with a range of practical suggestions will enable you to get real *use*, as well as fun, out of your home computer.

2 Computer Systems in the Home

When you first have your home computer, you will undoubtedly get a lot of fun from trying out the various games and standard 'routines' that are provided by the manufacturer. Apart from the thrill of seeing these run on your own machine, this initial phase is necessary to get to know what sort of things can be done with your newly acquired device. You will probably also buy some cassettes from stores that offer a range of games and other ideas. This off-the-shelf 'software' — the instructions for making your machine do a particular thing for you — will further widen your horizons about the potential of your home computer. By this time, you may have tried some simple programming, probably using the BASIC language, and in no time at all you will have the urge to make your machine do something exactly as *you* want it done. This is an exciting feeling which will never cease!

Your skills in programming will increase at every attempt. The problem is that you will be constantly looking for things for your machine to do other than give fancy, but rather trivial, demonstrations of its capabilities. You can of course try devising your own games, but in the long term *the real satisfaction of your home computer comes from making it do useful work for you*.

So how does one collect ideas for 'useful work'. I hope this book will go some way to suggest useful things for your machine to do and that it will trigger off many more of your own. But eventually you will be running up against day-to-day problems in your home environment which suddenly strike you as potential candidates for 'putting on the computer'. At this point you will already be thinking in the way that 'systems analysts' do. These people are specialists whose job is to improve the way in which information systems work, often — but by no means always — involving the help of a computer. It is equally important to bear in mind that, in your particular case, it may well be much more convenient to keep your address book just as it always was — a tatty, handy-to-pick-up paper booklet — in spite of the fact that I put forward a project to produce a 'computerised' address book. The important thing is to define what *you* want and then see what potential solution best fits your needs. This may, or may not, involve your home computer.

How does one develop this skill of systems analysis? In the office, this activity can become quite complicated, but the principles are the same wherever they are applied. The problems and the solutions that relate to home systems are likely to be very different from those in the office or factory, but the method of approach is the same. This chapter and Chapter 3 are about that method of approach.

Let us take a good look then at applying the principles of systems analysis in the home. There are essentially four steps:

1. *Getting the idea.*
2. *Deciding exactly what is to be done.*
3. *Doing the practical work to turn the idea into a working system.*
4. *Checking the results.*

The main work is concentrated in steps 2 and 3, but the other steps are essential as part of a systematic approach to making good use of computer systems. The simplicity but elegance of this approach, which can — and should — be applied to all information systems, can be seen from the descriptions in Chapter 3 of the main elements of each of the four steps.

Before discussing the steps and the principles involved in some depth, it is useful to take a practical example to see how you can proceed step-by-step from the first idea to a working system. Let us take an example that is applicable in most households.

CHRISTMAS CARD LIST

Let us assume that you, like most people, receive annually a number of Christmas cards, perhaps between 20 and 60, and that you send out a similar number. This sounds a simple procedure, and it is, but there is almost always an 'information problem' that makes it more complicated than it sounds. For example, you may well meet difficulties with regard to:

Change of address.
Knowing from whom you received cards last year.

So your decision about whom to send cards to this year, and at which address, depends very much on your knowing all the facts. This is where your home computer can help very nicely! Let us run briefly through the four steps identified above.

Getting the Idea

You have the idea to 'put your Christmas card list on the computer'. But before proceeding with the detailed job of trying to create such a system, you need to consider if you can really do this yourself and whether or not it would be worth the effort. To answer these questions you have to visualise, quite roughly at this stage, how you think such a system could work. You will probably come to the conclusion that you need:

A list of names and addresses, which you keep up-to-date during the year as your friends notify you of any changes.
A way of noting on this list when you last received a card from each person named, possibly showing the three preceding years.

This would enable you to look down the list sometime in November and decide on a case-by-case basis to whom you will send a card this year. Now, if you feel this way of approaching the problem is reasonable, the implications are that you will need:

To create a list (a 'file') on your computer of names and addresses with the additional information on cards sent, etc. You may see no special problem here, though you will have plenty of minor problems the very first time you try!
A means of keeping this file up-to-date. This sounds (and is) a standard job for any computer file.
A means of inspecting each name and address, with its additional 'Christmas card' information. Again this seems to be a relatively standard requirement, namely to be able to read the information you have stored in a computer file.

So, given some minimum experience, you will probably decide that the job can be done, without great difficulty. But will the effort needed be worth it? This is always the most difficult question in any decision to develop an information system. However, you can guess that the collection of the data (20–60 names, addresses and other information) will not be too difficult and that writing the necessary programs will not be very time-consuming (this you can judge only after having written some *working* programs). Your main problem will be to assess the usefulness of the system when it is working. If your present approach is very effective (perhaps based on a list on a piece of paper, or just keeping last year's cards), then you may well be doubtful. If, however, you have a problem every year in November in deciding on your cards, regularly get some 'surprise' cards, have difficulty in finding the addresses of some of your friends, etc., then you will very probably feel that a systematic approach to the problem would be very welcome indeed! On such a subjective, but nevertheless reasonable, basis, you will decide therefore to go ahead and have a go at developing a simple system to handle your Christmas card list.

Deciding Exactly What is to be Done

Before you can make anything work on your home computer, you have to be quite clear and specific about what it has to do. This would appear to be a burden, but it is really a marvellous benefit of working with computers. There is no room for ambiguity and you have to think through the whole problem and its solution before you can commence the subsequent step of programming. The latter requires skill, but the analysis and design work before is equally demanding and important.

So you proceed to define exactly what you want from your 'Christmas card system'. You therefore first consider the *output* you are seeking. You might well feel that ideally you want to be able to look at each name and address on your list, with the information visible to you in the following form (sample case):

Cards Received and Sent

	Last Year	*Year Before*	*Year Before That*
Mr and Mrs J. Smith	sent	sent	not sent
2 Woodland Road	not received	not received	received
Cherriford			
Herefordshire HR9 7BE			
United Kingdom			

This would be probably enough for you to decide that, since you had sent a card to Mr and Mrs J. Smith for two years running but received none in that time, you will this year not send them a card.

If you are satisfied that this is the information you want, you have in fact designed your 'output' — probably to be displayed on the screen of your home computer, though you may also have a printer. However, this has also defined certain other requirements, namely what data needs to be put into the system — the *input*. In this example, the input required is:

Name and address.
Yes/no indications of whether you sent a card to this name and address for each of the three previous years.
Yes/no indications of whether you received a card from this name and address for each of the three previous years.

You know therefore that you have to collect this information to build a file, keep it up-to-date and be able to look through the file at individual names and addresses. In fact, you now know what your *processing* requirements are, too. In this case, these are relatively simple, though there are some important guidelines to follow to ensure you do not lose the information by accident, etc., but these general design considerations are dealt with in more detail in Chapter 5. So far, you have been able to define quite clearly what you want for output, input and processing, and indeed how your system will work. What is still missing are the quantitative aspects, such as:

How many names and addresses you expect
How often you will need to make changes to these names and addresses

and a clear, written description of how you intend to do the job. This latter aspect is important both for proceeding to the next step (doing the practical work to turn the design into a working system) and for checking much later on what you have achieved, compared to what you aimed to do.

Also still missing is the detailed design work, such as defining exactly how your file of names and addresses, etc., will be organised, but again this can be accomplished using common techniques that are discussed later in this book. You are in principle now in a position to proceed to the next step.

Doing the Practical Work to Turn the Design into a Working System

Although your design is straightforward, there is quite a lot of work to be done to create a working system. There are two main activities to be carried out before you can begin testing the system — this itself being an important and often time-consuming activity. To bring yourself to that point of 'system testing', you first need (1) to create the file of names and addresses and (2) to write the computer programs that are necessary for making the system work.

Creating the file of names and addresses means collecting, organising and checking every name and address that you consider should be included. You will undoubtedly find that some addresses are incomplete, that some you cannot find at all and that you cannot remember whether some of them sent you a Christmas card last year or the year before, etc. In other words, you will be very lucky indeed if you are able to put together an accurate, complete list! But creating an initial file is a well-known, very common problem in all types of computer system. You simply have to do the best you can and aim to clean it up gradually (for example, by adding postal or zip codes) in the course of time. Once you have a reasonable set of names, addresses, etc., you can create a file on your home computer — provided of course that you have also by now written the necessary computer programs.

Writing the programs for your information system will dominate the work in the early days if you have not previously programmed a computer. However, as you gain experience, you will find that this occupies a decreasing proportion of the overall time spent on the development work for your home information system. In this particular case, a straightforward approach of writing programs would be suitable:

1. A program to create your name and address file.
2. A program to update the file.
3. A program to enable you to look through the file, inspecting each name and address.

It is possible to combine programs 1 and 2 or programs 2 and 3, but the simplest possible approach would be to keep three separate programs.

You will of course test each program as you write it, but it is only when you are satisfied that each works as it should that you will find the unexpected occurs — they do *not* work when functioning as a complete system (for example, when you try to update the newly created file, the program will not "accept' the data). This is also perfectly normal! System testing (that is, checking out the whole series of programs and data) usually throws up some inconsistencies in these programs and/or data. Some advice on system testing is given in Chapter 7, so we shall assume at this point that your system does work. And this being so, you will experience a very satisfying feeling indeed!

Checking the Results

A very worthwhile step is to let the information system you have developed settle down for a while and then take another look at it. In the case of your Christmas card list, this really means reviewing it after the first Christmas period. For systems that are used more frequently, it is best to let them run for several 'cycles' before checking them. The purpose is to see whether the system is working properly, whether it is useful and what improvements could be made. If you are disappointed to the extent that even improvements would not over-come the problems, then it is best to cut your losses and put the time you have invested down to experience and simply abandon the system. Hopefully, this will not happen very often and you will be well satisfied with the result. One of the surprises you may meet is that, while you yourself consider that everything is working well, other persons involved may feel that it is too much bother to go and use the computer to put in a new address, etc. This may mean you have made a design error (one should be able, if one wants, to collect changes on a piece of paper without having to rush to the computer) or (more likely) that you have not spent enough time with the other persons, getting them involved in the system, teaching them how to use it and so on. Computer systems more often fail in these human aspects than for technical reasons.

The above description is probably a lot more detailed than you needed to grasp the basic idea. In order to help you later in this book to browse for ideas without having to read in such detail, the main idea and its system implications have been summarised on a single page for each project. Such a page should be enough for you to decide whether or not you are interested enough to proceed to your own detailed analysis and design, as described in Chapter 3. The sample system described above would therefore appear as shown on the following page.

Home Computer Project — No. [1]

TITLE
Christmas Card List

BASIC IDEA:
To maintain a list of people to whom
you wish to send Christmas cards.

MAIN POINTS FOR SYSTEMS ANALYSIS AND DESIGN:

The decision whom to send Christmas cards to is often a complex one, but
this system can help quite a lot. It requires a simple file which records each
year the names of people *to* whom you sent cards and *from* whom you
received cards. Usually, a record for the past three years is sufficient. So,
around late-November each year, you inspect the file and make your decisions
name by name, at the same time updating the file accordingly.

LIKELY PROGRAMS:
To create the file.
To update the file.

To display each name and address and its associated information.

Although it is common to combine 'create and update' in the same program,
in this case it may be convenient to update at the time you are looking at the
file, item by item.

OTHER REMARKS:
This simple system could be
made part of a more general

'address book' system, but I think it is best used as a stand-alone aid for your
Christmas card problem!

3   The Key Steps

Having examined a particular example (the Christmas card list) in some depth, we are now in a position to review more closely the general principles mentioned at the beginning of Chapter 2. There we identified four steps that are common to the development of all computer information systems. This chapter therefore describes these four steps in some detail and in Chapter 4 we shall take two further down-to-earth examples to see how the approach is applied in practice. Here, then, are the four steps.

STEP 1: GETTING THE IDEA

At first this will be difficult. It takes a little time to develop the knowhow to 'spot' potential new uses for your home computer. However, once the ideas start flowing, they never stop! Even in the very beginning, you should not really be short of possible project ideas — this book contains suggestions for about 24 — and even minimal contact with other home-computer owners will lead to other ideas. It is important to have a go at making just one system really work at an early stage, because of its value to the learning process, whether or not the system itself is good.

   An important practical aspect is to write down the ideas in a systematic way. This is valuable for two purposes. Firstly, you will rarely be in a position to start work immediately on a potential project every time you have an idea. So keeping a log-book of potential projects is sensible especially as in the course of time you will pick up ideas from other sources that may not be obvious as being useful to your particular environment at that time. Browsing through this source book of ideas subsequently, however, might well lead you to see a good opportunity for yourself. Secondly, once you do decide to try out an idea, you need a sensible way of describing the idea to help formulate what exactly needs to be done. A reasonable set of points for this description is:

Title.
Key idea of aim.
Brief description of how you envisage it will work.
Main output
Data to be used as input.
Rough estimates of timing and effort.

If the idea turns out later not to be feasible, then it is still worth keeping your description in your log-book of projects. You can learn a lot by re-reading about old projects you abandoned!

The completion of this initial step of getting the idea is a key decision point: whether or not you feel it is worth going ahead with all the design and other work that is necessary to bring even a trial system into operation. Hence you concentrate on balancing out the various factors affecting the probable useful-ness of the final system. The problem of course is that much of the assessment is necessarily based on rough estimates. You do not really know how many changes there will be every month to your address book, or how big your computer programs will be, or how much time you will save by using your home computer instead of keeping a paper record of your accounts, etc.

The main factors you will need to consider are as follows.

1. Can it be Done?

This simple question has many important aspects, on each of which you will need to reflect carefully:

Are your own personal capabilities up to meeting the demands implied by your idea? For example, if the programming looks complicated, then you may never achieve a properly working system.
Is the general design, necessarily very broad at this stage, clear in your mind? If you are confused about how the basic information-processing problem could be solved, then be very cautious about any conclusions that the system is 'feasible'.
Does your particular home computer have sufficient capabilities (memory size, printout possibilities, etc.) for the type of system that you have in mind? Beware of trying to create systems, which you have seen or heard of else-where, on your machine, without knowing the comparative strengths and limitations of the various machines used.

2. Will it Really be Useful?

There is a natural tendency among computer enthusiasts to assume that a computer-based system will be better than the 'old' one. But there are many factors to be considered, especially convenience. This is not just a question of whether the system itself provides the information in the way you want it, but also whether you are prepared to go regularly to the trouble of walking to the room where your computer is kept, whether you keep the files up-to-date, etc. A key point is whether you yourself will be the only user of the system. If not, then you must talk your idea through very thoroughly with the other possible future users. Their idea of convenience will probably be very different from yours.

3. Will it be Worth the Effort?

Even assuming that your idea can be realised and that the final product will be better than your present way of doing things, there is of course still the major 'trade-off' question of net benefit to be answered. In the case of home computers, the cost factor (dominant in most business computer applications) is relatively simple to answer; the direct costs are likely to be low, but your investment in terms of your time is very probably going to be large. Now you may be willing to invest the time — but this decision should be taken only with full awareness of the likely usefulness of the system. Four weekends invested to print your own Christmas cards is hardly a bargain!

The end of Step 1 is in fact a decision — whether or not to go ahead and 'develop the system'. There will in the long term be no shortage of good ideas for using your home computer, so it is best to shelve an idea rather than proceed with something that is vague in itself or uncertain in its usefulness. This is important advice. Have the courage to discard good ideas, in favour of better ones!

STEP 2: DECIDING EXACTLY WHAT IS TO BE DONE

If you are reasonably convinced that your idea will work well in practice, the next step is then to become quite specific about what you want the system to do for you. In general terms, you will already have the scheme mapped out in your mind, because this will have been necessary for you to have made the decision to go ahead at the end of Step 1. In order to design a working system, these general ideas have to be turned into firm, written-down, detailed requirements.

Most computer specialists use checklists to help them produce this so-called 'system specification'. For home-computing a very rigorous approach may be desirable, but would be less fun, so I suggest following a broader, but nevertheless systematic, approach. This is based on an apparently paradoxical sequence of concentrating on these three factors, in the order given:

1. Output.
2. Input.
3. Processing.

The logic behind this sequence is as follows. Firstly, you must decide what information you want *out* of the system when it is working. This is simply forcing you to start from the side of the ultimate user of the system and define what the system will actually deliver. You are then obliged to think of the second aspect, namely the data that must be entered *into* the system if the desired output is to be produced at all. The final logical link then is to work out *how* the output you want can be created from the necessary input data – in computer jargon the 'processing' required. Specifying what you want done to the input data to allow the output to be created is an essential part of this step, leaving aside for now the alternative means you could use for achieving this.

The main kinds of detail you will need to specify these three aspects (output, input, processing) are:

Description of each piece of data (numbers of characters, volume of each type of data, etc.).
How often you want the results.
In what format you want to read the results.
How often the data changes.
How the different pieces of input data can be combined or converted to create the output.

When you feel you have a good grasp of the above, then you are in a position to proceed to the design of your information system.

Designing the system is the focal point for the creative part of developing an information system for your home computer. If you are tackling such a problem for the first time, you are unlikely to come up with elegant or clever solutions. Indeed, your aim should be to produce something that *works*. Some important general principles to guide you are given in Chapter 5 and in the course of time you will become familiar with standard solutions to certain aspects of systems design. The main points to draw your attention to at this stage are:

Work first on the 'output' end and put down on paper practical, trial attempts at how you think the system might work. You might even have a go on your home computer at this stage with some 'sample data', just to try out how you will handle it.
Design your basic file structure. Sometimes you will want to use your home computer for doing calculations without the need for a permanent file of

data. This is fine, but the typical case will involve some basic set of data
(for example, payments made, sports results, recipes, addresses) which you
will want to use as part of your information system. File design is discussed
in Chapter 5 and is an important part of most information systems.
Decide how you will build the file of data, in terms of its first-time creation
and its subsequent updating. Be sure to include checks that pick up as many
errors as possible. Errors in your source data can produce only problems!
Define and design the computer programs that you need to write to do
various parts of the job you have identified, usually:

> File creation.
> File updating.
> Searching the file for the pieces of information that you need.
> Summarising and displaying the results.

Depending on the scope of your idea, some of these may be combined (such
as file creation and updating).

STEP 3: DOING THE PRACTICAL WORK TO TURN THE DESIGN INTO A WORKING SYSTEM

This sounds self-explanatory, but this is where you expend most of your time!
The work includes:

> Collecting the data (names and addresses, prices, menus or whatever you are
> using).
> Writing the computer programs.
> Testing the programs.
> Building your file(s) on your computer.
> Trying out the whole system.
> Keeping a paper file of what you have done.

This last part ('documentation' in the computer specialist's jargon) is very
important. By the time you get to the stage of trial running, you will have lots
of loose pages on which you have defined the system design, the program, the
input data, the method of processing, etc. — much of which will have been
changed as you proceeded by trial and error. In a business computer installation,
it is essential to keep a careful review of all changes. Because you are using your
home computer for fun as well as practical uses, you are unlikely to do that, but
it is good advice to keep all the documentation you can in a reasonably systematic form for each information system you develop. Imagine you lose your
computer programs or your modifications do not work (a not uncommon
occurrence) and had to re-think everything again . . .

STEP 4: CHECKING THE RESULTS

Most home-computer users forget about this last step. Yet this is where you can learn a lot and ensure that your home computer is really being put to good use. The idea is to take a hard look at each information system that you have developed at any particular time when it has reached stability. Problems and overenthusiasm are typical in the first few months of use of any system. But the real test comes only when the system has reached 'normal' running. At this point, you should prepare yourself for a shock, because it is quite common to find:

That the system is being used much less than you expected.
That even though it is being used, the more traditional methods (such as an appointments diary) are being used in parallel to the new one ('electronic diary').

You will of course need to know why the situation has arisen. To help you approach the job systematically, the following items will give you a basic checklist:

Does the system perform as planned (too slow? not reliable enough?)?
Are there too many errors?
Do the back-up procedures work (when things go wrong)?
What do the other users think about: main benefits,
                                        main problems?

The purpose of this analysis is to provide answers to the following two questions:

What can be done to improve the system?
Should the system be scrapped?

It pays to be very realistic about the decision relating to the latter question. You will have gained experience even if the system is not working well or not being used much; to keep it going against the natural inclination of its users, for whatever reason, will be counter-productive in the long term. Computer systems are only useful if people genuinely feel the benefits and pursuing a less-than-satisfactory system may well prejudice the success of future efforts. So if you (and the other users, if any) are not satisfied, and there is no reasonable way to overcome the deficiencies of the system, then — abandon it! But let us hope that will not be the usual case. There are lots of good uses for your home computer. In the next chapter, we look at two more of them.

4 Some Sample Systems

In this chapter two more examples of a different kind are taken. By applying the broad ideas developed in Chapter 3, we can better see the kind of work that needs to be done in order to achieve some practical, working 'systems'.

FIRST EXAMPLE: CAR MAINTENANCE

As another example of how your home computer can be made to work for you, let us take the case of keeping a maintenance record of a car. Your inspiration for doing something like this could well be an uneasy feeling that your car is costing you more than it should do, or you may simply be curious to monitor its history in order to judge best when it would make sense to trade it in for something better.

So in *Step 1 (Getting the idea)*, you try to visualise whether it is feasible or not as a project and whether or not it could really bring you benefit. This will be more difficult than devising a Christmas card list, because the problem itself is much hazier. You will have to consider very hard what it is you want the information system to do for you. There is a danger that your ideas will be over-ambitious at this stage and that later (during Step 2) you will need to be more restrictive. It is best to focus on the critical aspect of your idea — I would suggest that you are above all interested in *costs* and that a complete technical record is of secondary importance.

You will certainly decide that a basic file will be needed, into which the cost and technical data will be inserted. You will probably already see the difficulty of describing in a precise way the reason for each expenditure incurred; indeed this is an early warning to keep the system simple! The other essential element clear to you will be the need to ask questions of the file and to obtain summary statements such as 'How much was spent on routine servicing from January to June last year?'

Your conclusion at this stage can therefore be summarised as: 'This idea is in principle straightforward enough and would provide me with very useful information. But I must be careful not to be too ambitious in the type of data I want to include, or I will meet lots of difficulties in collecting and classifying the data in a sensible way'. This positive, though cautious, position at the beginning of the first stage of a computer project is quite common and it is only during the next step that the real potential and associated problems fully emerge.

In *Step 2 (Defining exactly what is to be done)*, therefore, you are forced to make lots of apparently small decisions, which together in fact make up the system design as a whole. This is an important point. Although you should certainly have a broad design in mind, the scheme that emerges from the definition and design process in Step 2 is the sum of a multitude of individual trade-off judgements. Each of these should therefore be treated very carefully, not only in terms of its specific value but also in view of the cumulative effect on the overall design. For example, you might decide to treat 'replacements of electrical equipment' as a single cost category, but that would imply that you could not distinguish between routine replacement of a worn-out battery and of a smashed headlight – hence you are immediately limited in your ability to separate normal running costs from capital replacement costs. Of course, you could build in a special 'indicator' to specify for each item on your file whether it is a running cost, etc., but the example illustrates that apparently minor technical options in fact have much greater implications than appear at first sight and should therefore be treated accordingly.

At the completion of Step 2, you should have a clear picture of *exactly* which information you want out of the system. You will therefore need to write out on paper a complete sample result, of the kind:

Summary of costs (£)

Time period: January–June

Miles covered: 4000

Routine services	95
Petrol	150
Insurance	80
Non-routine repairs	160
Total	485

This may be all you want from your system, in which case your data definition is an easy one – only four categories of cost. But you might, as in the above example, be tempted to take a harder look at the unexpected figures (in this case 'non-routine repairs'). If so, you will want a listing of these in order to see what caused the high figure. Now, over a six-month period you will certainly remember what those repairs were – but over two years? And this will probably also point to the need for a comparative report over time, for example:

Summary of costs (£)

	This year to date	Last year	Previous year
(Miles covered)	(4000)	(10 000)	(9000)
Routine services	95	350	250
Petrol	150	300	200
Insurance	80	150	140
Non-routine repairs	160	140	30
Totals	485	940	620
Cost per mile (p)	12.12	9.40	6.89

If you do want to inspect each category in detail, then you will need to be able to display something like:

Summary of costs
— Non-routine repairs —

Time period: January–June

Miles covered: 4000

Battery	12
Seat-belt	15
Tyres	50
Re-spray wings	83
Total	160

This would appear to be helpful information and you could decide to go deeper and deeper, but at some stage you must draw the line or you will have a complicated system to program and to keep up-to-date in terms of the data-collection process. For example, it would seem reasonable to be able to produce the last table above for the current year, but is it really useful to keep information at this level of detail for previous years?

Deciding *exactly* on what information you want out of the system is essential in Step 2, as is *specifying the data* to be collected and stored in a file. This should follow naturally from your definition of the 'output' you require. But there are additional problems here. Firstly, not all the data you collect and need for your analyses will necessarily appear on your computer screen or printed paper — you may well summarise (within the computer system) some of the data you collect, such as petrol costs. Hence it is only at this stage that you may meet problems of defining exactly the kind of data you will collect. Secondly, you will now face in-depth the problems of 'coding' the data to be collected. This will in essence have been solved when you defined your output, because it was then that you decided on the categories of cost, time periods, etc. Nevertheless, you now have to devise as simple a scheme as possible for describing each category of cost. For example, your computer programs will have to be able to identify 'Re-spray wings' as a 'Non-routine' cost. The simplest approach is just to allocate a unique symbol (such as 'N') to each 'Non-routine' cost element (and 'R' for 'Routine services', etc.). The temptation is to combine this identification process with the means of describing the type of job (for example, 10 000 service). Again the level of detail will depend on the output you have specified, but in principle you could use the first digit of the job number to indicate the category of cost. For example, '1' would represent 'routine servicing', '2' 'petrol' etc. You could then build up a coding scheme, with other digits representing different kinds of cost: for example, the second digit could be '1' meaning 1000 mile service, '2' for 5000 mile service, '3' for 10 000 mile service, etc. Again the trouble is: where do you stop? You could end up with a very complicated scheme indeed! It is best to keep the design as simple as possible and use only the minimum number of categories. 'Meaningful' codes have been the cause of many a problem in using computers, especially when changes are needed (such as adding categories of cost). I suggest you do use a simple mnemonic code for the major categories of cost ('P' for petrol, etc.) and just a sequential non-meaningful number for specifying the exact type of job. This list you can store in the computer itself, for handy reference when inputting new data, and for adding to when you come across a new kind of car repair.

The third kind of design problem to be tackled at this stage is to define your file content and organisation. A file is made up of a number of items of information, which must be organised in such a way that your computer program can search systematically for a given piece of data or a given set of related data (for example, costs of replaced tyres). You therefore need to decide on what is going to be your basic 'item' of information and what exactly will go into it. In the case of a car-maintenance file, this could conveniently be each expenditure that is incurred. Each time a job was completed, a new set of costs would arise and these would be added to the file, which would gradually take on an appearance like:

Oldest item   Latest item

Data on 5000 mile service	Data on petrol bill	Data on re-spray job	Data on 10 000 mile service	Data on petrol bill	Data on insurance bill	

Each item of data will need to follow some completely defined structure, so that your computer program can find exactly what it is looking for. A possible structure might be:

Date	Type of cost 'R' = routine service, 'P' = petrol, etc.	Type of job	Number of miles on the clock	Cost

Note that 'Type of job' is not needed for all categories of cost (petrol, insurance). This structure assumes that you have one car; if you have more than one, you could add a special 'box' that gives the registration number — or create separate files. Assuming you have decided on the type of output discussed above, then your computer programs will summarise data for a given period of each type of cost. So the programs will be 'looking for' the 'date' and 'type of cost' and will add up the actual costs incurred for each. The difference between the 'number of miles' for the items having the earliest and most recent dates gives the 'miles covered' for the period being analysed.

Much of the thinking work will necessarily have been done by the time you move to *Step 3 (Doing the detailed work)*. Nevertheless, it is at this stage that you will meet many practical problems, such as:

Meeting data that does not seem to fit into your file design.
Difficulty in programming and getting the programs to work.

These types of problems are minimised through good design work and it is well worth spending extra time and care in Step 2 in order to avoid difficulties at the implementation stage. In the case of a car-maintenance information system, you will have to put quite a lot of work into starting your file with good, coded data, writing the programs, testing the programs separately on 'test' data, testing the programs on real data, testing the programs in conjunction with each other, actually using the system on a routine basis, showing others how to use it, finding errors long after you thought it was in good order, etc.

From the above, you will gather that it is quite normal to meet lots of problems when you are at the stage of turning your idea — however well-defined — into a working system. Experience will also show you that, whereas these problems can usually be overcome, it is prudent to assume that some errors will always remain in the system and that lots of things can happen to cause problems (power cuts at awkward moments, losing bits of paper with important information on, interruptions while you are updating the file and so on). This brings up the question of security.

You should be able to recover from most situations without a major effort. This implies keeping copies of your file and programs in a safe place and ensuring that the original data (the garage bills) are kept until your file has not only been updated but used — these are just examples of security measures to prevent loss of all that time, effort and valuable data you have invested. Good security starts at the design stage (in Step 2) and continues throughout — and even beyond — the life of an information system. The principles and practice of security are very important and therefore this aspect of home-computing is dealt with explicitly in Chapter 5.

Reviewing the problems as well as the benefits is one of the main purposes of *Step 4 (Checking the results)*. You will want to reflect on whether or not the information that you now have is really helpful to you (and possibly others), whether or not the system is reliable, whether or not it is too much work, etc. You will probably find that you wish you had tackled the problem somewhat differently, for example by using broader categories of cost data or by having more totals available to compare different types of job, different years, different cars, etc.

Your difficulty will be to decide which aspects could be improved within your working system and which are so fundamental that only a re-design could really solve. A general guideline is *not* to introduce major changes at this stage. If the system is working, only minor improvements should be attempted, for example by letting the computer add up a certain set of figures to give an extra 'total' figure. Even this will probably cause surprise errors when you try it out. Trying to introduce a new category of cost could be very troublesome indeed.

Whatever you decide to do in the end, the review process is always worthwhile. It helps you gain the maximum possible from your practical experience. Although your car-maintenance information system may not benefit greatly from Step 4, your next system undoubtedly will!

As in the first example described in this book, the basic idea of the car-maintenance information system is described for handy reference on the summary sheet on the next page.

SECOND EXAMPLE: MAGAZINE SUBSCRIPTIONS

By now you will be familiar with the general approach of systems analysis and design for your home computer. Hopefully, the example described so far in this chapter will have helped you relate the principles discussed in Chapter 3 to the practical work involved. This book contains outline descriptions of over 20 more possible projects and the purpose of the second example in this chapter is to point the way for you to take up some of these other projects in your own environment. So, the starting point this time is the summary description sheet, Home Computer Project — No. 3, entitled 'Magazine Subscriptions'. This gives a bare outline of the idea and you may like to use it as means of proceeding through the 4 steps of systems analysis and design.

In Step 1 (Getting the idea), therefore, you will probably want to narrow down the broad idea suggested. For example, the objective on the summary sheet includes the idea of controlling payments of subscriptions. This,

Home Computer Project — No. [2]

TITLE

Car Maintenance

BASIC IDEA:

Each time your car goes for maintenance or repair you record details of
what work was done and what it cost. This enables you to build up an accurate
picture of your car-maintenance problems and costs. This information is
useful in lots of ways, such as comparing garage charges, working out the cost
of running your car, judging when to sell your car, predicting likely bills,etc.

MAIN POINTS FOR SYSTEMS ANALYSIS AND DESIGN:

Your system analysis will need to focus on what data you want to collect. You
will quickly identify the essential data (date of service, mileometer reading,
cost, main job done, etc.) but the difficulties will be:

To devise a simple identification and coding scheme for the work carried
out on the car (such as 010 for 5000 miles service, 020 for 10 000 mile
service, 030 for new tyre, 040 for bodywork re-spray, etc.).

To design a logical format for the data elements you decide on and to
formulate convenient 'keys' for finding the data when stored on the
computer (suggestion: use 'date' and 'type of job').

The other main point will be to decide on what type of information you
will want *out* of the system at any one time. You might simply want to
display a complete record of a given service, but you will probably want
also to have some summary reports such as total costs over a given period
of time, cost for a given type of job, etc.

If you have more than one car, the simplest approach is to establish a file for
each car, but you could identify each car (by its registration number?) and
use the file to make some interesting comparisons of costs.

LIKELY PROGRAMS:

You will need a program to
create and update the file(s);
this should be straightforward. But for your program to find and display the
data will require much more work, depending on how sophisticated you want
the information to be.

OTHER REMARKS:

Although simple in its basic
idea, this system can be made
quite comprehensive (and difficult to program, if you try to be too clever!).
But it can lead to real savings by indicating a change of garage or car, etc.

Home Computer Project — No. ⬚ 3 ⬚

TITLE
Magazine Subscriptions

BASIC IDEA:
To keep track of your subscriptions to magazines, journals, newspapers, etc., so that you can control payments and plan renewals.

MAIN POINTS FOR SYSTEMS ANALYSIS AND DESIGN:

The best way to organise this system is on a monthly basis; that is, any time you inspect the file it shows you at a glance the subscriptions that are running out that month. You should also of course be able to select any other month for inspection.

Two additional features to build in are:

(1) When a subscription is paid, you want the file to reflect this. This implies that the file must cover a period of 24 months or more. Also you may want to record detailed transaction data (date of payment, cheque number, etc.), but you will not want this to appear on the screen every time you select a month. So you also need feature (2) below.

(2) Apart from selecting by month, you will also want to select according to the title of the magazine or journal. This would then enable you to inspect the complete history of your subscription for this magazine. So, in spite of the fact that the main system concept is a monthly one, your file is in reality a series of detailed records for each magazine. During the actual 'run time' of your programs, the relevant information is then assembled for you, depending on the type of request you formulate.

LIKELY PROGRAMS:
You will certainly need programs: To create the file.
To update the file (for example, when paying a subscription).
To display the data you want. Here you will need to build in the two basic options of displaying a 'month' or 'magazine title'. Note that, if you organise your data into records about each magazine, then asking for a given month implies that the program examines every record in the file.

OTHER REMARKS:
Although the above refers to a system for controlling magazine subscriptions, you can of course apply a very similar approach for monitoring your membership of clubs, professional associations, etc.

however, makes the system much more complicated. If your main objective is simply to monitor your subscriptions, then a straightforward file that you can inspect monthly is sufficient. But if you would like to be able to check conveniently on when you made payments, then of course you need to be able to update the file regularly to reflect this. In Step 1, therefore, it is important to be sure of your objectives and prepare an outline of a system that would meet these, without straying into side-issues that could greatly complicate your work.

Step 2 then consists, as in the previous examples, of being quite specific not only about the objectives but about the detailed way in which the system must work to fulfil them. Again, you will need first of all to be quite clear about the *output* you want. Apart from the possibility of including payments, you will need to consider what kind of question you will be wanting to answer when using the file. You may well decide that you would like to see responses to such questions as:

What subscriptions will need to be renewed in December?
When did I start subscribing to this magazine?

These two simple questions imply immediately that you will want to be able to inspect the file to gain the complete picture (1) for a given *month* and (2) for a given *magazine*. So your program(s) for handling the file must be capable of extracting information in at least these two ways and providing you with the information in a neat, consolidated presentation. There are many other questions you might want to ask, such as 'How much did I spend on magazine subscriptions last year?' But beware of being too clever! Although that question would be relatively easy to cater for, it would also be simple to answer the question 'How much have I spent so far this year on magazines A, B and C?'. If you try to provide for too many optional questions, you will end up with difficulties at the programming stage. Concentrating on the essentials is an important element in a disciplined approach to systems design.

The effort in Step 3 (Doing the detailed work) will be directly related to the complexity of the definition and design you have settled for. Your work will anyway focus on:

Collecting the relevant data for each subscription that you currently have running.
Writing a program to create and update the subscriptions file (these could be two separate programs).
Creating the file (and updating it if, as usually happens, changes occur while you are still developing the system).
Writing a program to find and display the information you want.
Testing the programs and use of the whole system generally.

At some stage you will decide that everything is working satisfactorily and you will then view the system as being 'operational'. It is important that this is a conscious decision, because systems that are truly operational can settle down and become part of normal life; systems that are in a constant state of development or undergoing improvements can never really be relied upon or accepted by the user.

After a few months of normal usage, it will be time to undertake Step 4 (Checking the results). Only then can your efforts be really assessed. The good and the bad points are best seen in perspective well after the running-in period. Your magazine subscription system will hopefully appear in a favourable light and you will be tempted to apply the same approach to other types of subscriptions (clubs, professional associations, etc.).

5 Design Factors

By now you will have recognised that certain questions and issues occur again and again whenever you plan a new use for your home computer. For example, in almost every case you need a collection of data — a file. This file has to be organised in such a way that you can find the information that you need, often in a variety of different forms. Another aspect that arises regularly is defining the output in a precise way, to enable you to work out the format of the displayed information and, very importantly, to find exactly what information needs to be put *into* the system.

These and many other factors arise almost every time you design an information system. It is useful therefore to develop some general guidelines on how to tackle these recurring design problems. Fortunately, the basic principles of computing are very much the same whatever the size of machine and whatever the environment. The business and academic worlds have invested enormous amounts of effort and expertise in the use of computers and today there is a large store of experience on which to draw. From this experience, the principles described in this chapter are of particular importance to the home-computer user.

1. GENERAL DESIGN PHILOSOPHY

Apart from certain specific design factors of the recurring type (discussed in the second part of this chapter), some general principles can be of great help to you in developing a sound approach to the design of information systems on your home computer:

Aim for Idiot-proof Systems

Every good designer of information systems assumes that 'the user' — the person who will actually be expected to handle and make use of the information system — will *not* be able to use the system properly. That is not to say that you should adopt a superior attitude towards the user, but rather that no user should be expected to know all the intricacies of the system. In fact, the system should show *resilience* to mistakes. The onus should be on the designer to anticipate potential problems that may arise.

Now, if you are the only person who will use your home computer, the problem is of course much reduced, though you will be surprised how often you press the wrong button or cannot remember what to do next. If others are going to use your system, then the chances are that they will do things you never even dreamed of, let alone believed possible! The important element in your attitude of mind as a designer is that it is *your* fault, not the user's, if something (not always accidentally . . .) upsets the system. So, for example, in your design, always provide a 'please help me' mechanism that allows the user to gain immediate guidance from the system itself (for instance by pressing the question mark key, or keying in 'HELP'), whenever he or she is in difficulty. Then you must also assume that data will be lost or wiped out occasionally, so you always have a back-up copy of the data (part 2 of this chapter gives some specific advice on this aspect). These are just examples of the design philosophy of aiming at idiot-proof systems. A friend of mine once remarked that in the design of information systems the case where the system is used in the normal way is a trivial one — the skill lies in anticipating the wrong ways in which the information system will be used!

Keep It Simple, Stupid (the KISS Approach)

This heading will probably be familar to readers with engineering backgrounds. 'KISS' has become an axiom of good engineering — including information-systems engineering. The basic principle is that complicated solutions tend to lead to errors in systems design, during implementation and consequently in the use of the eventual system. *The simpler a system is, the greater is its chance of success.*

Furthermore, the inevitable modifications that need to be made during the normal lifetime of any information system are notorious for triggering off errors if the system has been designed as a 'clever' one.

So, in practical terms, never hesitate to write two programs rather than one, if that simplifies the problem; leave super-subtleties, however intriguing they may appear as an intellectual exercise, out of practical working systems; play safe when you are in doubt whether a particular feature will help or confuse the user; and so on.

A simple system that *always* works is much, much better than the clever one that works 99.9 per cent of the time!

Design Modular Systems

One of the biggest mistakes a designer of information systems can make is to create a system as a single unit in which everything is so interlinked that a small change in one part of the system triggers off multiple changes (or errors!) else-where. The concept of modular design is to divide the 'problem' (the information system you are seeking) into separate parts, as far as possible manageable in their own right. This aids:

Understanding of the problem.
Formulation of good alternative solutions.
Introduction of modifications to the system, during development or subse-quent operation, with minimum risk of causing other changes and errors.

How then do you apply this obviously desirable, but rather general approach, in practice? There are two key guidelines for applying modular design:

Structure your design ideas into logically separate units. Examples of this are: treat the creation of a file as a separate problem from its subsequent updating; use several small separate files, rather than one or more 'integrated' files; devise separate methods for finding the data you want and for displaying it.
Have as few links as possible between the different parts of your information system. The idea here is that a 'module' (for example, updating a file) should be virtually a stand-alone unit. So you can run your update program and stop there for the time being if you so desire. If you want to do something with the updated file, this can then take place as a distinct activity on its own. The advantages are many, including flexibility in running your information system, reduced effect of modifications to programs or data, etc. Ideally, a module can be created, tested and used independently of other modules. Although it might not be meaningful to do so, this does give rise to the possibility of using a module developed for one purpose (such as input checking of sums of money) in a different system at a later stage. The interconnections between individual modules are largely defined by the input and output specifications for those modules.

2. SPECIFIC DESIGN ASPECTS

Data and File Handling

This topic lies at the heart of the detailed design process of information systems. In commercial data processing, quite sophisticated and sometimes very complicated methods are used to 'manage' the data in as effective way as possible. The term 'data base management system' is in common use and is an indication of the importance allocated to this aspect of using computers. It is important too in the use of home computers, but fortunately the size and number of your files are likely to be much less than in a commercial environment and the full range of data base management techniques is less likely to be useful. Indeed, there is so much 'overhead' involved in managing large data bases that you will probably be much more efficient with your home-computer system than is possible with very large systems. The basic principles, as one might expect, are largely applicable no matter what size of system and this section examines the essential points to be borne in mind.

Input validation

It is only when you have had experience of running a 'live' information system that the importance of having accurate and complete data becomes evident. A computer program that tries to do a calculation with a letter 'I' rather than the digit '1' will soon run into trouble. It is best to avoid this sort of problem by doing as much checking as is reasonably possible before erroneous data reaches the stage where it can cause problems. The following steps are all sensible measures to take as part of the input and validation process.

Check the data manually before it is fed to the computer.
Although you cannot hope to spot all errors and deficiencies, a quick inspection by yourself of the data you plan to input can help a lot to pick up such points as: unreasonably high numbers, missing elements in a name and address, alphabetic letters in the middle of a number, etc. Wherever possible, it is best to check a batch of similar data on the same occasion; this will not of course always be feasible but the eye becomes accustomed to identifying patterns of data and so finds anomalies more easily in repetitive checking.
Separate the input checking from the processing.
Again, this is not always possible (for example, when you are doing certain types of interactive computing), but it is a good general principle, nevertheless. The idea is to sift out — and if possible re-enter in corrected form — the erroneous data before it is handled by the main programs. This can be applied in practice by:

Making the initial creation of a file a separate process from its subsequent updating. Although creating a file can logically be combined with updating, there are usually many more errors and omissions in the original data used to form a file than later additions and changes. It is therefore a good idea to set out to create a clean file before working on the means of updating. In programming terms, this implies separate programs, which can apply different types of checking procedure.
Structuring your programs so that the input checking parts are logical

units that are separate from the rest of the programming. These input-checking parts become stand-alone 'routines' to which data is referred before it is processed.

This principle is a natural consequence of the modular design concept, discussed in the first part of this chapter.
Ensure that each piece of data is checked at least once.
There are many types of control you can apply, but the most common are:

Reasonableness checks (is the data within the normal limits of possibility?).
Digit/alphabetic checks (certain pieces of data, such as a price, should not contain alphabetic characters, just as a person's name does not normally have any numbers in it (though there are rare exceptions!).
Sum totals (for example, when you input items on a bill, the computer could check that their sum corresponds to that shown on the bill).
Counting checks (if a number should contain a minimum number of digits, such as a telephone number, then your program can check this; also you might specify that there are bills for 12 months to be input and the computer can remind you if you have input 11 — or 13!).

As you gain experience, you may be tempted to apply more and more controls to the input data. You should bear in mind, however, that 'over'-control is as bad as insufficient control — it costs time in processing and uses computer memory space. The benefits at a certain point follow a rapidly diminishing returns curve. Furthermore, the convenience factor plays an important role; whereas serious errors must be stopped, minor ones (such as two spaces between words instead of one) do not normally matter enough to risk irritating the user.

File organisation

The principles of developing information systems on your home computer are (and should be) almost independent of the type of machine that you have available. The topic of file organisation is, however, influenced to some extent by what type of facilities your particular home computer has for storing data. It is not a question of a specific manufacturer or model but of the 'configuration' — the jargon word used to describe the exact mix of processing possibilities that a specific computer has. Apart from a central memory (RAM — Random Access Memory — available for your programs and data, plus ROM — Read Only Memory — used by the computer for its own processing needs, including handling your programs) it will certainly be able to operate with cassette tapes. These you will use regularly for storing programs and data. But you may also have discs or discettes, which allow you to access data in a more flexible way than cassette tapes. The latter, by their nature, store data *sequentially* and this characteristic determines the way you organise your files and the way your programs handle them. However, if you also have discs (and the equipment for these is much more costly than for cassettes), then your programs can find data that is physically located in the middle of a disc, without having to 'read' through all the preceding data. This opens up considerably more possibilities for you in the way you set up and use your files. These are discussed later in this section.

Whatever possibilities you have for storing and finding data, the basic unit is in principle always the same, namely a 'record' -- a group of data items forming together some logical set of information. An example of a 'record' is: name, address and telephone number. It is often convenient to visualise this in a simple way, such as:

Name	Address	Telephone number

(sample contents of a 'record')

When planning the organisation of a file, you can then add other details about this record, for example:

Name	Address	Telephone number

| Up to 30 alphabetic characters and full stops | Up to 100 characters, some numeric, some alphabetic, plus punctuation | Up to 15 numeric characters |

You can (and will need to) proceed to even greater detail (for example, exactly how is the telephone number constructed — area code, then number?). Another example might be:

Name of magazine	Address for paying subscription	Date for renewal	Price of annual subscription	Date of last payment	Amount paid

If you keep a file of your magazine subscriptions, then you would have a series of records:

Name of magazine (1)	Address etc.	Amount paid	Name of magazine (2)	Address etc.	Amount paid	etc.

Whether or not you physically string these together on cassette tape or on a
disc depends on what your computer offers and on how you have decided your
programs will use the file. Let us look, then, at the options. There are three basic
types of file organisation.

Sequential files
This is the normal way you would store data on a cassette tape. Each time you
make a mortgage payment, for example, you might update your 'mortgage
file', which could be represented as follows:

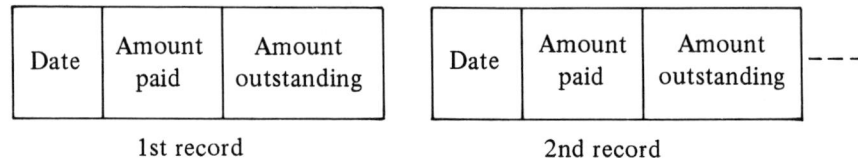

	1st record				2nd record		

| Date | Amount paid | Amount outstanding | | Date | Amount paid | Amount outstanding | – – – |

Here there is a natural sequence to the records — namely, date. But some sequential files have no 'natural' order, such as a name and address file. Others can be
placed in meaningful sequences, according to the use you have in mind. Let us
take the example:

Date	Repair job on house	Cost

You might want simply to list the data in chronological order, that is, by date.
You might, however, be more interested in adding up costs by type of repair
(for example, exterior painting) over a given period of time. Now you can
program in such a way as to be able to meet either or both of these requirements,
regardless of the sequence of the records. The program simply 'looks at' each
record in turn and either displays it or adds up the appropriate costs for each
category. But there are cases — one of which is a key part of most information
systems — where the sequence is very important indeed. The critical case in point
is *updating* a sequential file, but this is just a particular application of the more
general case of handling two files simultaneously. If you intend to update only
one record, or very few, at one sitting, then an out-of-sequence file does not
matter too much. But if you want to save your amendments until they are
sufficient in number to warrant setting up the system to update the file in
'batch', then you really want to feed your amendments into the computer
in the same logical sequence as that used by the file itself. For example, a name
and address file might look like:

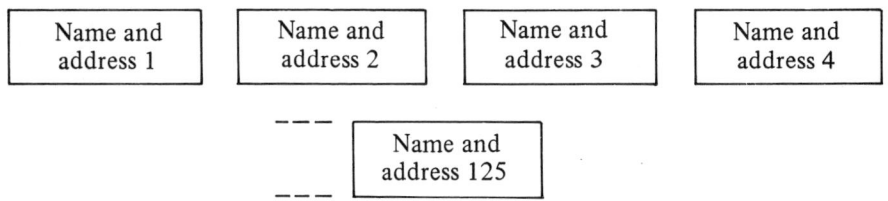

If you have amendments to name and address record numbers 3, 19, 21, 43, 62, 89 and 111, it is clearly more efficient to take these amendments in exactly that sequence, matching each record by 'name' before changing the address, than to introduce the amendments in the sequence 62, 19, 111, 3, 89, 21 and 43. The latter would mean that your cassette tape holding the file would have to be read up to the point where record 62 is found, the change made, the tape rewound and then read again up to record 19, the change made, read further to record 111, the change made, rewound, read forward to record 3, etc. Having both amendments and file in the same basic sequence means that the file simply advances from record 3 to record 19, to record 21, etc., with a rewind occurring only once, when the job is finished. This principle of having two sets of data in the same sequence is fundamental to sequential file organisation and allows updating and 'merging' (combining) of files to take place efficiently. Schematically, this can be represented as in Figures 5.1 and 5.2. The method of representing information-handling processes by diagrams such as those used in Figures 5.1, 5.2 and 5.3 is known as 'flowcharting'. This topic is dealt with separately in Chapter 7.

If File 2 is not normally kept in the same sequence as File 1, then an initial step — called 'sorting' — will be necessary to create a special version of the file in that sequence. The procedure would then look like that shown in Figure 5.3.

This sorting would depend entirely on a given data item, called a 'key' in computer jargon. For example, if File 1 was your main name and address file, it would probably be ordered alphabetically according to each 'name'. File 2 might be a 'bills paid' file, however, with the sequence determined by date, such as:

earliest   latest

Date	Nature of bill	Amount	Name and address of supplier		Date	Nature of bill	Amount	Name and address of supplier

record 1   record 62

To update File 1 using File 2, the latter would need to be sorted using 'Name and address' as a key, to put the 62 records into a sequence that is purely dependent on the alphabetic nature of each name.

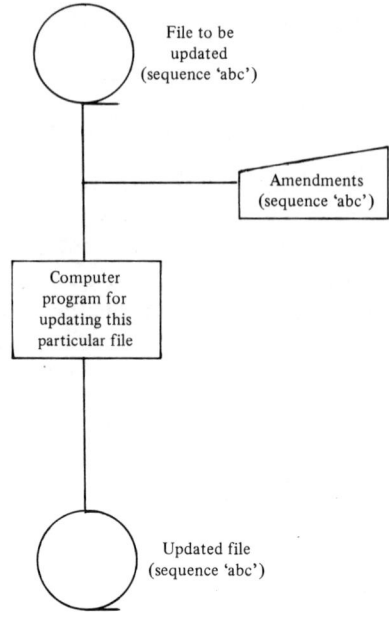

Figure 5.1   Updating of a sequential file

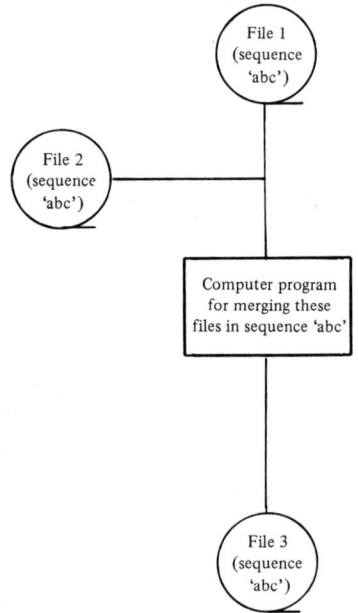

Figure 5.2   Merging of two files

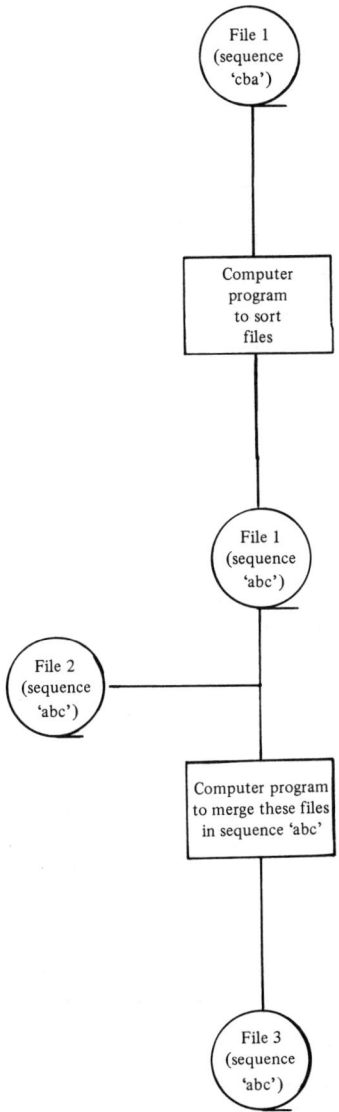

Figure 5.3   Sorting and merging

This process of handling data in various ways by sorting and merging opens up many possibilities for your home computer as a real aid to your information needs. You should *not* need to write the programs for sorting a file, as these should be provided with the system when you acquire it.

Random file organisation

Disc systems offer the possibility to locate a piece of data within a file without having to read sequentially through much of the other contents of the file. Many of the restrictions of sequential files (for example, sorting before updating when dealing with multiple amendments) are thereby overcome. Data can be changed *in situ* without having to be copied on to a new cassette.

The means of locating a given piece of data is normally by means of a 'dictionary'. This records the physical location of a piece of data within a file in conjunction with some identification of the record (for example, magazine name). So when a program needs data on a given magazine, it refers to the dictionary in order to be able to find the data on disc.

Naturally, there is a cost associated with the use of such file techniques. Firstly, the devices needed to operate discs are much more costly than those for cassette tapes. Secondly, for efficient use, the dictionary needs to be in main memory, during use, and this costs valuable memory space. Thirdly, although the retrieval process is much faster using discs, the storage of data is less efficient generally than for cassettes, since vacant areas begin to develop in the disc (owing to occasional 'overflow' problems and the need to leave some free space). Also the constant need to refer to the dictionary can result in slow processing for some types of application.

List structures

This type of file organisation is an attempt to combine the best of sequential and random organisation. The individual records are distributed randomly on disc, but each record contains a 'pointer' (the physical address) of the next related record. This implies a sequence of records and you may well ask what the advantage is over a pure sequential approach. The answer lies in the fact that each record can have multiple 'pointers'. So the sequence relating a series of records can vary according to which pointers are being used.

List structures are very powerful and can be developed to a high degree (for example, pointers can become the main file with the actual record contents representing a minor part of the data volume!). They can as a consequence be costly in storage and processing time. Nevertheless, as home-computer systems increase enormously in storage and processing power, it can be expected that list processing and other forms of data-management tools will become standard parts of the software provided. At the present time, however, the average home computer is restricted not so much by the cost of the disc units but by the lack of supplier software to allow you to make proper use of them.

Retrieval ('Find and Display')

In the two preceding chapters it has been stressed that the systems design process starts with defining what *output* is required. Most of the information systems that you are likely to develop on your home computer will include some facility to find and display a piece of data that is located within a file. Although the exact details will vary according to the file and the nature of the information system, there are some general considerations which can be used in designing this 'find and display' process, known in computer jargon as 'retrieval'.

Format

In deciding on what output you want, you automatically must be visualising roughly how the data will be laid out on the screen or paper printout. It is best to make this visualisation process a deliberate, concrete step with pencil and paper. The immediate purpose is to force yourself to be precise about the output you want, but in so doing it is common to discover that you have not thought through the implications of your idea, for example, by designing a display such as:

Golf Scores on Home Course

January	95
	92
February	92
March	93
	94
	96
	89
April	87
	98
	88
	89
	91

Average this year to date: 92

Average over last 12 months: 94

The number to be inserted in the 'Average over last 12 months' clearly requires a rolling average. While this is simple to program, it does imply that it is calculated each time the program is run and, more importantly, that there must always be data available for each of the preceding 12 months. The number required is not 'Average for last year', a constant figure, but a changing figure with definite requirements at the file-content and program-design levels. This simple example is intended to illustrate that focussing on format and exact specification of the output at an early stage is an essential activity for good design.

Searching

If you are using an indexed file, then your programs will gain direct access to the data being sought. But in sequential and simple list structure files you (that is, your programs!) will need to 'search' for a given piece of data. The field of search strategies generally is a big and often complex one, beyond the scope of this book. It is possible here only to give some basic guidelines for efficient searching:

Try to bring in as many records as possible from external storage into central memory before searching. This minimises the time lost as a result of the relatively slow (compared to central memory) speeds of input/output devices. Pure sequential searching (examining one record after another as they come in their file sequence) is feasible only if (1) the file is small *and* (2) the frequency of accesses to the file is low. Remember, the average number of records looked at before finding the one you want will be half the number in the entire file! A method of searching a sequential file that can save a lot of time is so-called 'binary searching'. In spite of its name, it is a very simple process. Imagine a series of records ordered 1 to 50 as follows:

If you look first at the middle (or near middle) record (no. 25) and compare its value to the one you are seeking (let us say number 15), it is very likely to be higher or lower in value than the one you want (in this case higher) — unless it just happens to be the exact one, in which case you have found it in the shortest possible time! If it is higher in value, then you immediately look at the middle one of those lower in value, that is, no. 12, and again examine it for a 'high–low' comparison:

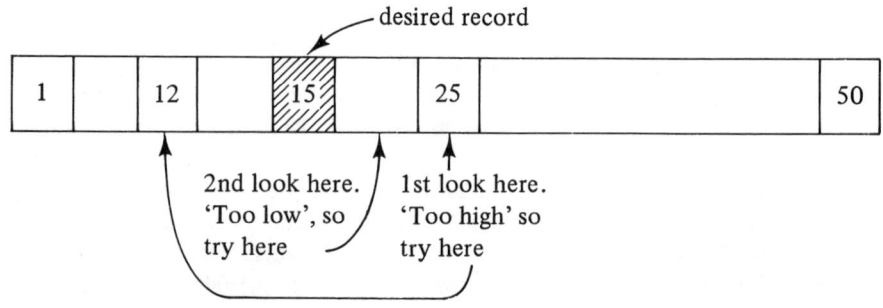

And you proceed further in the same way until you find the record you want:

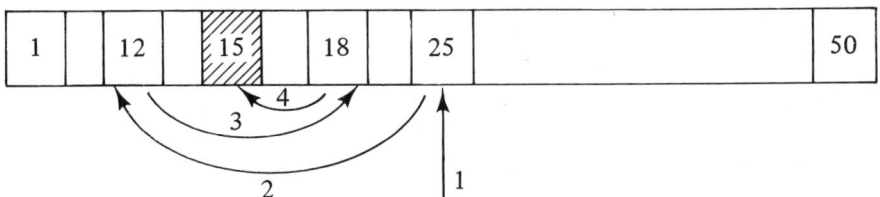

This is a way of rapidly 'homing in' on the record being sought. The average number of accesses to find the record will of course increase with the size of the file but compared to straight sequential searching it represents an enormous saving for large files.

Search 'language'

In Chapter 8, the concept of 'user friendliness' — trying to make the system simple and convenient to use — is discusssed in detail. Nowhere is this concept more important than in the process of helping the user find the information he or she wants. The instructions given to the user must be:

Very clear so that messages are unambiguous and not too 'telegram-like', which can be irritating to the user. For example, messages such as 'REPEAT INPUT' are not very helpful!
Self-explanatory. It is tempting to give a list of options at the start with such statements as:

'PRESS T IF YOU WANT TOTAL'

or

'LP MEANS LATEST PAYMENT'

These may save storage or screen space but are not very effective if the user cannot remember later what 'LP' means. Ideally, one wants to be able to understand any message without previous experience or reference to some list or other; in practice, this is difficult to achieve, but this goal should be kept in mind at all times when designing the search process.
Helpful even when the user is totally confused. Hopefully, your message will not confuse the user (!), but even the best systems can sometimes lead to situations where the user wonders what on earth to do next, either because he or she has simply forgotten the next step or because of erroneous input. There should, therefore, always be an 'escape' route. This means that the user can at any time indicate to the system (for example, by keying in 'HELP') that he or she is lost, and the result should be clear guidance from the system

as to what to do. This can be a simple reminder of what the alternative steps are or a statement of where the user has got to and what is expected next. If the user still does not know what to do, a more basic explanation should be offered — and so on, until the ultimate case of starting again completely from scratch (as if one had just switched on the system) is reached. *Considerate* to the experienced user. Giving lots of help to the user is very desirable — provided it is wanted! That is the idea behind this point. Experienced users do not like constantly to be reminded that they can press 'HELP' if they make an error, etc. It is wise therefore to allow experienced users to bypass the detailed explanations available, either by letting them identify themselves as such right at the start or by giving fast options at each step.

Security

Dependence on an information system has long been recognised as a vulnerable point in business and other organisations. The home is equally vulnerable in its own way. Though losing your diary, complete with addresses, may not have immediate survival implications, it is still a serious incident for most people. Unless there is a complete catastrophe (such as the house burning down), the risk of losing your diary plus bank statements plus club membership records, etc., is small, however. The concentration of your information sources on a home computer is therefore a new risk factor, which deserves careful attention. The following three basic principles are given here to help you devise appropriate security precautions.

Apply general security measures for your home-computer system.
A computer system in the home is just as vulnerable as any device, so you will need to take basic precautions with regard to the usual hazards (fire, theft, etc.). Apart from the computer itself, your programs and data (on cassette tapes or discs) are equally vulnerable and it is important to keep these well labelled and safely stored. The convenience of access to your home computer is an essential condition for its usefulness, but this does tend to expose it to physical mishaps and to temptations from casual 'button-pressers' who cannot resist having a go. Even with the very best of intentions, this can cause problems and it is wise to assume that sometimes the computer will go wrong. For this reason, each individual information system dependent on your home computer should have some precautions of its own, as described below.

Build in security for each information system.
The importance of ensuring that errors in the input data are, as far as possible, spotted and corrected before processing starts has already been emphasised. This is one form of 'system control'. However, there are many others that can be applied within the processing and output processes, too, for example, simple checks on:

Numbers of items being processed.

Totals (individual sums corresponding to the sum of sub-totals, etc.).

Checking that records match not only on one item (such as name) but also on other unique information (such as telephone number).

Ensuring that the first and last records on a file are handled properly (a frequent source of errors).

In addition to these measures, which take place at the programming level, the manual checks on the information finally received are of course the ultimate form of control. The user's feeling for reasonableness of the information provided is a critical check and the confidence in the result depends on this.

Assume the worst will happen !

Whatever precautions you take, once in a while something will happen that you had not anticipated. But assuming that this itself will happen is already a considerable help, because it brings to you the importance of *recovery and insurance*. Recovery here is meant to describe the process of getting back to normal again after something has occurred to upset the system. This may be a physical defect in your computer (implying delays for repair), losing a program tape with its copy, having a program error that wipes out a file, etc. Any one of these may represent a low risk, but the chance that one of them will occur from time to time is high!

You should therefore always provide for a 'recovery procedure'. This means a combination of precautions. You will need to arrange with a friend or other person with an identical (or fully compatible) home computer to yours to be able to run your program and files on his system, if necessary. This necessity is not likely to arise often, but it could be that you urgently need to know details of your insurance payments just when your system has broken down. It is also a good idea to arrange with a friend to keep copies of programs and files in each other's houses. The files may not be fully up-to-date, but a back-up copy of a fairly recent version is sufficient to prevent the catastrophe of total loss (in the event of fire, etc.). Your programs themselves should as far as possible limit the effects of breakdown or error; this is a further benefit of the modular design approach discusssed earlier in this chapter.

Finally, it is worth considering to what degree your normal insurances cover potential losses relating to your home-computer system. You may be primarily concerned with the equipment costs, but as time goes on you are likely to have invested very much more in the creation of programs and data. Furthermore, the vulnerability factor becomes important when you reach the stage of depending heavily on your home-computer information systems. Insurance can never be the total answer — basic security should be built into the systems themselves — but can be a useful complementary measure for major risks.

6 More Sample Systems

Here then are some twenty or so summaries of possible applications for your home computer. It is unlikely that every one of them will appeal to you, but hopefully some at least will trigger off good ideas of your own. Each application is presented on a single page. For quick reference, here is a complete list, including the three presented earlier:

Project No.	*Title*
1 (in Chapter 2)	Christmas Card List
2 (in Chapter 4)	Car Maintenance
3 (in Chapter 4)	Magazine subscriptions
4 (projects 4–24 are presented in this chapter)	Diet Plan and Weight Record
5	Recipes and Menus
6	Hobby Index — General
7	Hobby Index — Example 1 (Reading List)
8	Hobby Index — Example 2 (Sports Scores)
9	Hobby Index — Example 3 (Wine List)
10	Football Pools Forecasting
11	Examination Question Spotting
12	Mortgage Payments
13	Homework Schedule
14	Diary
15	Insurance System
16	Heating-Cost Monitoring
17	Address Book
18	Transport Timetable
19	Family Tree
20	Checklists
21	House-building Control
22	Hotel and Restaurant List
23	Family Medical History
24	Teach Yourself Systems

Home Computer Project — No. [4]

TITLE

Diet Plan and Weight Record

BASIC IDEA:

To record a given diet and monitor your weight loss

MAIN POINTS FOR SYSTEMS ANALYSIS AND DESIGN:

In its simplest form this information system gives you a day-by-day account of the meals specified on the diet and the weight reading. However, the system becomes much more interesting if you add to it other pieces of information such as date (diet success can vary by time of year), extra or less food and drink taken than prescribed by the diet, general comments (tiredness, stomach problems, etc.). These will together form an interesting record of the whole diet course, which may help you when you apply it on some future occasion. Also if you record each different diet course in this way, you will have a fair means of comparison to select which diet suits you best.

LIKELY PROGRAMS:

A program to create an open-ended (indefinite time period) file of the diet itself.
A display and update program, for use each time you use the file.

OTHER REMARKS:

Be honest with the information you put into the system on your weight loss, 'sins', etc.!

Home Computer Project — No. [5]

TITLE
Recipes and Menus

BASIC IDEA:
To keep an 'electronic notebook' of ideas for cooking recipes and menus.

MAIN POINTS FOR SYSTEMS ANALYSIS AND DESIGN:

You could simply specify a file of cooking recipes and design some straight-forward form of retrieving these under logical headings (starters, desserts, etc.). However, you could also introduce a creative approach, whereby complete meals (say, a starter, a main course and a dessert) are proposed. This will of course require plenty of cooking knowhow (which types of combination are acceptable or unacceptable) and some careful programming. If you entertain a lot, you may also find it useful to keep a record of what guests have been served what dishes.

LIKELY PROGRAMS:
To create and update the recipe file.
To find recipes and possibly propose meals.

OTHER REMARKS:
This information system
is not only for fun — it is really useful!

Home Computer Project — No. [6]

TITLE
Hobby Index — General

BASIC IDEA:
Many hobbies involve systematic collection of information (for example, collecting stamps or antiques, reading, knitting, bird watching, etc.). This system is designed to help you keep an index of the information that you collect.

MAIN POINTS FOR SYSTEMS ANALYSIS AND DESIGN:

The main feature of this system is a file (or set of files) that stores in a convenient way either (1) the information at the heart of your hobby (such as names of birds and dates sighted, etc.) or (2) an index to information (such as references to books, articles, etc.). Your main difficulty will be to define exactly what you want in the file. Although there may be a temptation to build one large, complex file, it would be better to establish several different, simpler files, for example, one file for books on your hobby field and a separate one for your collected pieces (such as antiques).

LIKELY PROGRAMS:
A program to create each file and update it will be needed.
Do not start to write these programs until you are quite sure exactly what information will make up the files, in what format it will be stored and what you are likely to want to do with the files.

A program to 'manipulate' the information in whatever way you want, such as list stamps by country, or by value or by age, etc.

OTHER REMARKS:
The above description is intended to draw your attention to the possibilities generally for using your home computer as an aid to your hobbies. The Home Computer Projects on the next few pages give specific, practical examples.

Home Computer Project — No. | 7 |

TITLE
Hobby Index — Example 1 (Reading List)

BASIC IDEA:
Whatever hobbies you have, most of them will involve reading of books on the subject, or reading generally itself may be your hobby. Some books you will purchase, some you will borrow and some you will want to acquire or borrow some day. This index helps you keep track of what you have read, what you have on your bookshelves and what you want to read next. It helps overcome those frequent uncertainties of:

(1) What authors to look out for in bookshops and libraries.
(2) Whether you have read the book before, possibly under a different title.
(3) Noting new titles when you hear of them.

MAIN POINTS FOR SYSTEMS ANALYSIS AND DESIGN:

This system could be made quite sophisticated, but I suggest you concentrate on the following:

Decide on what your main uses of the system will be, such as listing all books by a given author, retrieving individual books by title, just browsing.

Define a record to describe any book in terms of your interest (such as AUTHOR, TITLE, PUBLISHER, DATE OF PUBLICATION, ISBN, TYPE OF BOOK, DATE PURCHASED, DATE BORROWED, COMMENTS, etc.).

These two pieces of work should enable you to decide on the best file organisation and structure for your purpose and on the exact form of output required.

LIKELY PROGRAMS:
File creation and update program.
General-purpose display program.
Listing program.

OTHER REMARKS:
This is likely to become popular with different members of the household. You could simply keep separate files for each person, but you might consider an integrated file based on identifiers for each person.

Home Computer Project — No. [8]

TITLE
Hobby Index — Example 2 (Sports Scores)

BASIC IDEA:
Whether an active player or an armchair sportsman, most people who follow some sport as a hobby would like to keep a record of the performances of themselves or of their favourite teams, players, etc. This system is meant to give you an idea for keeping a simple information system on one or more of your favourite sports, be it billiards, football, darts, golf, etc.

MAIN POINTS FOR SYSTEMS ANALYSIS AND DESIGN:
Your main difficulty will be to decide just how comprehensive you want your Sports Scores information system to be. You could, for example, decide simply to record your personal golf scores; but even here many possibilities are available — do you include the name of the course in the basic record, whether a twosome or foursome, etc.? As this concerns a hobby area and therefore a 'fun' job, I suggest you design something simple to start with, say a basic record of information with a straightforward retrieval method. Then, through use, you will get further ideas for its enhancement and you can either add bits to the system or re-design it completely. This is not recommended practice normally! But assuming you do not mind investing effort into your hobby, a pilot scheme is a useful way to find out your real needs. You may end up with quite a sophisticated system, enabling you, for example, to calculate a moving average of your scores.

LIKELY PROGRAMS:
The usual file creation, update and retrieval programs will be needed. But you are also likely to invent other ones to meet special-purpose requirements (for example, calculating averages, plotting trends graphically, etc.).

OTHER REMARKS:
Hopefully, the above is sufficient to trigger off other ideas for the monitoring of your personal sports interests.

Home Computer Project — No. | 9 |

TITLE
Hobby Index — Example 3 (Wine List)

BASIC IDEA:
This is a system for keeping an inventory of something you collect. Example 1 was concerned with a book list, but this example goes further. Firstly, the information stored is more comprehensive and would include original price, present value, earliest and latest dates for drinking, etc. Secondly, you want the system to reflect your consumption or sales of the wine, plus possibly comment on quality.

MAIN POINTS FOR SYSTEMS ANALYSIS AND DESIGN:
Again your focal point will be the contents of the file. These of course will depend on what you want out of the system. As indicated above, the system is just a simple listing approach, but one that handles quite a range of information and in which the individual records will undergo updating. So you will need to consider updating procedures (source information for the change, volumes, frequency of updating, etc.).

LIKELY PROGRAMS:
The usual set of file creation, updating and display programs will be needed, plus possibly an occasional listing (on the screen, or on a printer, if you have one) of the whole file. You may want this listing program to do other things, too, such as giving totals, like 'total value', and grouping by type of wine.

OTHER REMARKS:
You are hardly likely to develop this system if you do not keep (or drink!) a fair amount of wine, but it is illustrative of a more general type of use of your home computer — the system could keep an inventory of anything you collect.

Home Computer Project — No. | 1 0 |

TITLE
Football Pools Forecasting

BASIC IDEA:
This is a natural offspring of the project on Sports Scores. By systematically recording football scores of the teams on pools coupons, you have the opportunity to apply forecasting techniques, which will hopefully improve your chances of winning!

MAIN POINTS FOR SYSTEMS ANALYSIS AND DESIGN:

The two main aspects are:

Setting up a systematic data-collection scheme in order to build a file of results. But do not decide on this part until the following aspect is quite clear in your mind.

Devising a forecasting scheme. The simplest approach would be just to display the relevant results history for a given pair of teams and leave the judgement to you of the next likely result. However, in the long run it will be less time-consuming and more fun to specify a set of rules for your home computer to make the forecast. Even for a simple set of rules you will need a systematic way to describe them before programming; for this, decision tables (see Chapter 7) are ideal.

LIKELY PROGRAMS:

File creation and update program.
Forecasting program.
Possible separate program to display selected parts of the file.

OTHER REMARKS:
Since the forecasting program could be quite complex from a 'logical rule' point of view, it is best to start with a modest approach and not be too ambitious at the start.

Home Computer Project — No. [11]

TITLE
Examination Question Spotting

BASIC IDEA:
To help preparation for examinations by analysing topics set in previous papers, in order to forecast a likely set of questions.

MAIN POINTS FOR SYSTEMS ANALYSIS AND DESIGN:

This has a natural affinity to Project No. 10 on Football Pools Forecasting! You will need to define exactly a scheme for classifying (and coding) each type of question and for what period you will collect this information (say, 7 years). You can then design a file to which your question-spotting analysis can be applied. This question-spotting is a forecasting exercise, somewhat simpler than for football matches, though examiners do of course deliberately aim at avoiding regular patterns of questions. Nevertheless, for many situations (O- and A-levels, end-of-term tests, etc.) quite simple techniques are effective, based on plotting the time interval after which a given question becomes very likely.

LIKELY PROGRAMS:

File creation and update program.
'Browsing' and display program to allow you to inspect the file.
Question-spotting program.

OTHER REMARKS:
This system is only worthwhile if you plan to use it for more than one set of examinations. My first system took more of my time for development than I suspect it was worth — I could have better spent the time doing comprehensive study for the examinations!

Home Computer Project — No. | 12 |

TITLE
Mortgage Payments

BASIC IDEA:
To monitor mortgage payments and to evaluate effects of changes in the interest rate, tax structure, etc.

MAIN POINTS FOR SYSTEMS ANALYSIS AND DESIGN:

You could use your home computer just as an accounting aid to keep track of mortgage payments, calculating the amount outstanding, etc. But it would be a pity to limit it to this, since it is fairly easy to include also the possibility to calculate the effect of changes of, say, the interest rate on your monthly payments.

LIKELY PROGRAMS:

To create and update the payments file.
To calculate results of changes in interest rate, etc.

OTHER REMARKS:
There are standard formulae for calculating compound interest, but you may like to work out your own method, possibly by simple iteration (that is, calculating the long way but using the speed of your computer).

Home Computer Project — No. | 13 |

TITLE
Homework Schedule

BASIC IDEA:
For anyone following an educational course, whether at school, technical college, university or evening institute, this system will help you plan your homework, by providing a schedule of homework obligations, plus recording marks achieved, etc.

MAIN POINTS FOR SYSTEMS ANALYSIS AND DESIGN:
It is best to start by defining exactly what the homework schedule will look like on the screen. The layout and content will give ideas for using the file in other ways than simply updating and looking up the schedule. Once this aspect has been decided upon, the data required, and the means of entering, storing and retrieving it can be specified.

LIKELY PROGRAMS:
Program for creating and updating the homework schedule file.

Program for examining the file and possibly doing analysis on it (for example, average marks per subject, etc.).

OTHER REMARKS:
This is a good project for a new home-computer user to start with.

Home Computer Project — No. [14]

TITLE
Diary

BASIC IDEA:
To keep an up-to-date schedule of all your private commitments, such as dentist's appointments, vaccination shots, passport renewal, holiday dates, visits of family and friends, birthdays, anniversaries, theatrical bookings, sports events, etc.

MAIN POINTS FOR SYSTEMS ANALYSIS AND DESIGN:

The first point to consider is how you wish to display a 'page' in your diary. This implies deciding on:

Time span (day? week? month?) for the basic display.
Format of the displayed output.

If you want to put quite a lot of information on the screen, then it is unlikely you will be able to display all this for one week at a time.

Secondly, you will need to decide how 'clever' your use of the diary is to be. Good effective use would simply be to display any given week (or day, or month). But you could exploit your electronic diary more fully, by having it respond to commands like 'display: dentist's appointments', or 'display: birthdays' for a given period. This of course would require much more detailed definition of how the data itself must be formatted, as well as more complicated programs.

LIKELY PROGRAMS:
Program to create basic diary format.

Program to input and update the diary information.   Display program.

(Note: You can buy ready-made software packages for 'electronic diaries' on microcomputers. So it is worth checking to see if one fits your machine and meets your needs.)

OTHER REMARKS:
Just as losing your private diary would be serious, so would loss of the electronic one. Security precautions are therefore essential, with back-up copies taken frequently (say once-a-week).

Home Computer Project — No. | 15 |

TITLE
Insurance System

BASIC IDEA:
To monitor insurance payments (and receipts). You can build in other features, such as identifying when an insurance needs to be upgraded (for example, fire insurance being affected by inflation) or degraded (for example, dropping comprehensive insurance from your ageing car).

MAIN POINTS FOR SYSTEMS ANALYSIS AND DESIGN:
From a systems analysis point of view, this project has similarities to the Magazine Subscriptions system (Project No. 3). The basic system requires a file that gives details of each insurance. Then at some appropriate interval (monthly is probably the most convenient) you obtain a display of those insurances that are due in the near future. You might also want to browse ahead, again on a month-by-month basis to help you anticipate cash-flow requirements. Then there are lots of features you could add, such as handling claims information, totals by type of insurance, etc, as well as those mentioned in the description of the basic idea above. The file for this system will be small but with complicated records.

LIKELY PROGRAMS:
Apart from your file creation and updating program you could end up with quite a demanding program for selecting information. A simple find-and-display program would be straightforward, but the more analyses you want carried out, the more (and rapidly) complicated this selection program could become.

OTHER REMARKS:
If you are relatively new to home-computing information systems, it is best to take the straightforward approach — display of monthly information plus display of individual records.

Home Computer Project — No. ⬚ 16 ⬚

TITLE
Heating-cost Monitoring

BASIC IDEA:
To keep a detailed record of home-heating costs. This is a straightforward cost-accounting information system, aiming to help you monitor your home-heating costs. These may depend on oil, gas, electricity, coal or other source, but the principle is the same, namely to record consumption and cost, with a view to obtaining guidelines on optimal ordering times and quantities, night and day temperature settings, trade-offs between two forms of heating (for example, electricity and coal), etc.

MAIN POINTS FOR SYSTEMS ANALYSIS AND DESIGN:
The basic output will be a summary report showing costs to date this year. These are only meaningful if you also show the costs for the same period last year. Because of fluctuating prices, it is best also to show the actual units consumed (such as, litres of oil). The production of this summary report will depend on a simple file of costs and fuel units and an early task in your design work must therefore be to decide on the exact content and format for this file. You can keep last year's figures in the same record, if you wish, or you can keep a separate file for each year and feed in both files each time you run.

LIKELY PROGRAMS:
File creation and input program(s). Report display program.
There is an opportunity here for some graphic representation (cost and/or fuel-consumption curves).

OTHER REMARKS:
The monitoring of heating costs is particularly useful because of the high costs involved. However, this is just an example of the type of cost-accounting approach that could be developed for any type of home expenditure.

Home Computer Project — No. | 17 |

TITLE
Address Book

BASIC IDEA:
Names, addresses and telephone numbers of all your personal contacts are stored in your computer system and kept up-to-date for easy reference.

MAIN POINTS FOR SYSTEMS ANALYSIS AND DESIGN:

You will probably want to use your file in the same way that you use a pocket book, that is, by looking up names alphabetically. So be sure and define the 'name' clearly, allowing for long names, initials, company names, etc. It is also a good idea to classify each address in some way, such as 'personal', 'hotels', 'restaurants', 'job contacts', etc., so that you can browse through each category separately (for example, when seeking a restaurant). If you want to be clever you can add other indicators, such as 'Christmas card recipient', but these can be dealt with in separate files, as described earlier. The more complicated you make your file, the more care you will have to exert in updating each entry and in designing your retrieval program.

Finally, be sure and take extra care over the security of your file (keep an up-to-date copy in a safe cupboard, etc.), because the inconvenience and cost of losing your address list can be very high indeed.

LIKELY PROGRAMS:
File creation and update program.

Retrieval program, (1) to find name and (2) to browse through a category of entries.

OTHER REMARKS:
If you are new to computer systems, keep your system as simple as possible and it will be of great value to you. Too clever an approach may mean that you spend a lot of time wondering whether it is working properly!

Home Computer Project — No. [18]

TITLE
Transport Timetable

BASIC IDEA:
To keep a personalised timetable for those parts of the public transport services used by you and your family. This is not an attempt to make your computer do something better than a set of standard bus, train and air time-tables. The idea here is to work out manually (using published timetables) those connections that are relevant to you and store them for family reference and updating. Routine commuters are not likely to need this system, which is meant more to cover the occasional trips to specific locations. A quick check on this system helps plan the trip.

MAIN POINTS FOR SYSTEMS ANALYSIS AND DESIGN:
The 'key' for using the file is the name of the location to be visited. In most cases, the departure and return base will be your home address, but there will be occasions when this is not so. It is therefore a good idea to build in the facility to specify both destination and starting point; for the case of 'home', some simple indicator (such as 'H') should be used. Some interaction will be needed to establish the exact parameters needed for giving the answers (for example, day of week, time of day, etc.). The output should display the options most closely meeting the wishes expressed.

LIKELY PROGRAMS:
File creation and update program(s).
Enquiry program.

OTHER REMARKS:
It is the combination of train, bus, etc., that makes this an interesting and useful system. The more combinations there are, the more useful the system is!

Home Computer Project — No. [19]

TITLE
Family Tree

BASIC IDEA:

To build a historical record of your family tree.

MAIN POINTS FOR SYSTEMS ANALYSIS AND DESIGN:

In its simplest form, this system just records births, marriages and deaths, but you can expand on this with all sorts of details, such as weight at birth, burial location, etc. Agreeing the contents of the file within the family can be very interesting! Whatever you do agree, you must assume that by no means all the information will in fact be available and that there will be large gaps, especially as you go 'back' in time.

For output purposes a graphic tree-like display is nice, just giving the simple relationships, though only about two generations can be conveniently shown on one screen. So you need some way to enable the user of the system to browse forwards or backwards in time. You will also want to be able to display a complete record for individuals.

LIKELY PROGRAMS:
File creation and update program(s).
Display the tree and browsing program.
Display a detailed record program.

These last two can conveniently be combined, as it is often the case that someone will want details when a particular person is located in the tree.

OTHER REMARKS:
Dog and other animal owners
will see the potential of this
system for other forms of breeding!

Home Computer Project — No. | 20 |

TITLE

Checklists

BASIC IDEA:

This is a simple application for your home computer, but it is put to very practical use. Just as you might keep a notepad for maintaining a checklist for any activity (for example, holiday planning, wedding presents, etc.), so your home computer can help you — and keep the list for future reference, if desired.

MAIN POINTS FOR SYSTEMS ANALYSIS AND DESIGN:

The effort for building a system to handle very short and short-term checklists, such as those for shopping, would hardly be worth it. So you will need first to be sure that there really is value in the result. This value may well stem from the usefulness of building up a checklist over a period of time, based on experience — for example, a checklist for camping.

If you make the decision to go ahead based on the likely value of the checklist data, your systems design work should focus on making it a general-purpose system. You justify your initial effort on a particular, say camping, checklist, but you should make it generally usable for gardening or Christmas planning too! Bear in mind that for some purposes the usefulness of the system is reduced if you do not have a printer to run off a copy of the checklist.

LIKELY PROGRAMS:

A file creation and updating program.
A listing (and, possibly, printing) program.

OTHER REMARKS:

This is an example of a general-purpose system for your home computer, starting with one practical case but ensuring it is usable for lots of purposes.

Home Computer Project — No. [21]

TITLE
House-building Control

BASIC IDEA:
Anyone who has been through the process of adding to or converting an existing house or building a new one will be familiar with the incredible amount of minor problems and delays that arise through the difficulty of planning, at least partly owing to lack of organised information. This system will certainly not guarantee optimal planning, but may help to relieve the stress involved by providing a reasonable central source of information in your building project.

MAIN POINTS FOR SYSTEMS ANALYSIS AND DESIGN:
Off-the-shelf program packages do exist for planning and controlling construction projects. Some of these can be used on microcomputers and it is worth looking at them if you are into building in a fairly major way. But the idea behind this simple system is just to provide a good file of information on costs, materials, contractors, etc., and to do the real planning and monitoring yourself! The latter can be built into the system to some extent, at least showing which activities and which materials have to be ready by given dates. A more comprehensive system would involve you in a lot of analytical and programming work. Even setting up the basic file is a problem — what logical basis do you use for the record? You could set up separate files for: materials; milestone planning; costs. Too many files will make the system cumbersome to use and I suggest you concentrate completely on those aspects of critical importance to you (probably cost rather than time).

LIKELY PROGRAMS:
These will depend on how ambitious your system is, but will very probably include at least (1) one file creation and update program and (2) status report of, say, time and costs. You may want to display a bar chart of time and costs.

OTHER REMARKS:
This is an interesting and potentially valuable use of your home computer, as quite straightforward information aids can save major costs (such as avoiding underordering or overordering, late ordering, delays in connecting to water and electrical supplies, etc.).

Home Computer Project — No. 22

TITLE

Hotel and Restaurant List

BASIC IDEA:

This is a sort of personalised 'Michelin Guide'. You keep a simple file of hotels and restaurants used by you, for handy reference when planning a trip or meal out.

MAIN POINTS FOR SYSTEMS ANALYSIS AND DESIGN:

The heart of the system is a record of each establishment that you want to be included. This record could consist of: name, address, telephone number, type of establishment (hotel or restaurant or both), price range (two sets of prices if it is both a hotel and restaurant), price you paid last time (give date), quality assessment, other remarks.

The find-and-display part can be as simple or as complicated as you wish. At the least, you should be able to specify location (town) and type of establishment (hotel or restuarant). Even then, looking for a restaurant in your home town could be time-consuming, so you might want to build in other factors too, such as price range.

LIKELY PROGRAMS:

File creation and update program(s). Find-and-display program.

OTHER REMARKS:

This straightforward reference list approach can be applied to many other types of information, for example, shops that stock certain goods.

Home Computer Project — No. | 23 |

TITLE
Family Medical History

BASIC IDEA:
To keep a record of family illnesses (such as measles, mumps) and other relevant information (such as allergies).

MAIN POINTS FOR SYSTEMS ANALYSIS AND DESIGN:

This system depends on a carefully built-up file. Because it concerns very personal data, you will probably want to restrict it to the immediate members of the family only. The content and quality of the data are clearly the central factors here, both from the point of view of medical importance and of personal privacy. The structure of the file is most naturally based on a medical record for each person (that is, a record is allocated for each individual). This means you must leave the record length and structure very open-ended.

The retrieval part of the system will be very simple — just display a record for a given person. You are unlikely to want to go to the trouble of writing a program that can answer questions like 'Who suffers from bronchitis?'

LIKELY PROGRAMS:
File creation and update program.
Simple display-a-record program.

These could easily be combined, though logically they are two separate activities.

OTHER REMARKS:
Security and privacy are important factors here, so be sure to keep a recent copy of the file locked away in a safe place.

Home Computer Project — No. [24]

TITLE

Teach Yourself Systems

BASIC IDEA:

The idea here is (1) to have some fun in trying your hand at computer-aided instruction and (2) to use your computer actually to improve your spelling, your French verbs, your mental arithmetic, or whatever you choose to try out.

MAIN POINTS FOR SYSTEMS ANALYSIS AND DESIGN:

Computer-aided instruction is a highly developed field that combines computing and pedagogic skills. You should not try to compete with such experts. But as a means to interest children and to brush up on rusty knowledge, this is a fun application of your home computer. There are ready-made packages available for some fields, so it is worth buying one or two of these to see the style of working. However, it is best here to adopt a simple approach, based on successive interactions between the machine and the user. Your initial attempt need not be long or complicated; testing say 10 French verbs or asking the user to spot spelling mistakes in a 20-word list is simple for a start, and can easily be added to later.

LIKELY PROGRAMS:

The programs for this type of application are fun to write, as they have to prompt the user (for example, 'DO YOU WANT TO TRY ANOTHER?' or 'THAT WAS VERY GOOD. NOW LET'S HAVE A GO AT A MORE DIFFICULT ONE . . .'). You will need to write a separate program for each subject you want to teach.

OTHER REMARKS:

This type of system is good for impressing your friends!

7 Useful Techniques and Methods

The professional computer specialist learns a range of techniques to help in the analysis, design and implementation of information systems. Some of these (for example, simulation) are more powerful than necessary in most home-computer applications. Some, however, can be very helpful in this environment and it is useful to be able to use them, when appropriate. The last phrase is important. It is by no means necessary to apply *all* the techniques every time you develop a new information system for your home computer. Part of the difficulty for the newcomer is not so much in understanding the technique itself but in knowing when and to what degree to use it. As far as possible, indications are given in the following sections of when and where to apply the techniques and methods described.

FLOWCHARTING

In Chapter 5, the discussion on file handling included some diagrammatic representations of the file-update and file-merging processes. These were in fact 'flowcharts'. Flowcharting is a highly developed technique used to help:

The systems analysis process.
The systems design process.
Program design.

Strictly speaking, the term flowcharting applies only to the first two of these and there exist international standards for the purpose. Similar symbols are often used by programmers in their work. For home-computer use it is quite sufficient to apply the *concept* of flowcharting in its basic form, without worrying too much about the full range of symbols available.

The way in which flowcharting can help you is perhaps best illustrated by a practical example (Figure 7.1).

If you update the master file on the console just before the selection and printing process, this would appear as in Figure 7.2.

However, you may wish to collect all your amendments for the master file

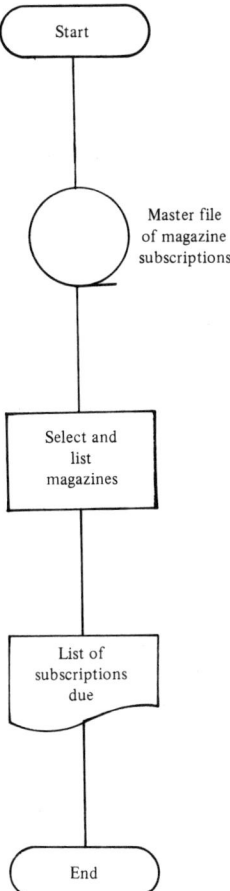

Figure 7.1   Flowchart: listing from a file

together and let the computer do the updating alone. This would require sorting into the correct sequence, so the flowchart would appear as in Figure 7.3.

In this way the various processes involved in information-system design can be described graphically. To do so with words alone can be clumsy, though of course by no means impossible. Flowcharting is a useful technique for working out design ideas and for expressing them clearly when you have decided on the approach you will take. It can then help you to identify exactly what programs are needed and help with the programming itself. The latter application is particularly useful when you have lots of different points in your program where there are alternative steps to be taken, depending on the particular case in hand. The example shown in Figure 7.4 is an illustration of the way flowcharting can help at quite a detailed level in programming.

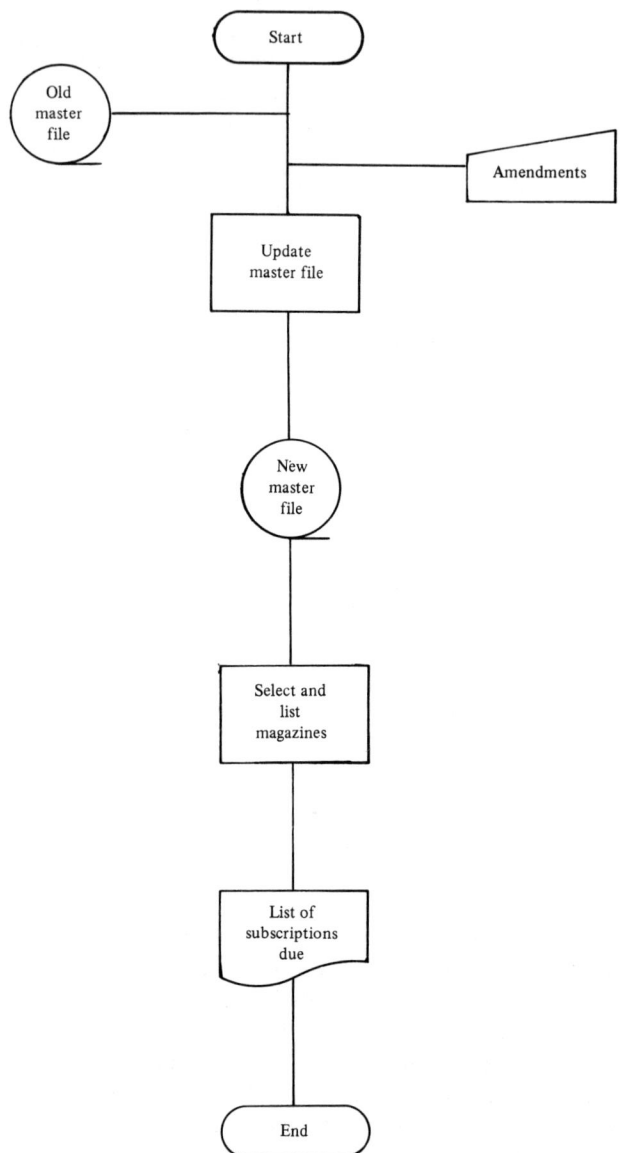

Figure 7.2   Flowchart: updating a file before listing

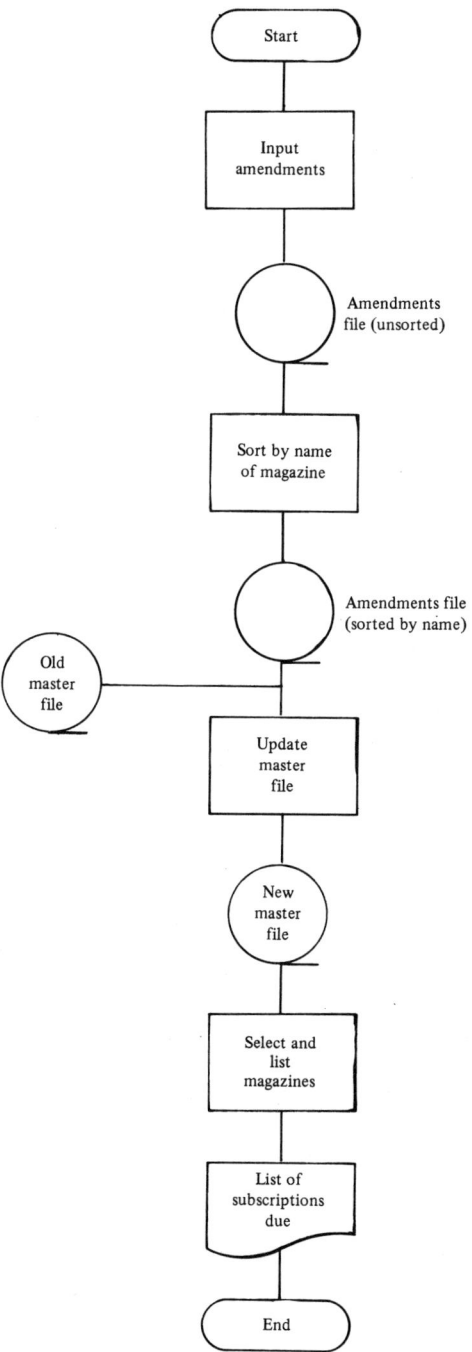

Figure 7.3   Flowchart: sorting, updating and listing

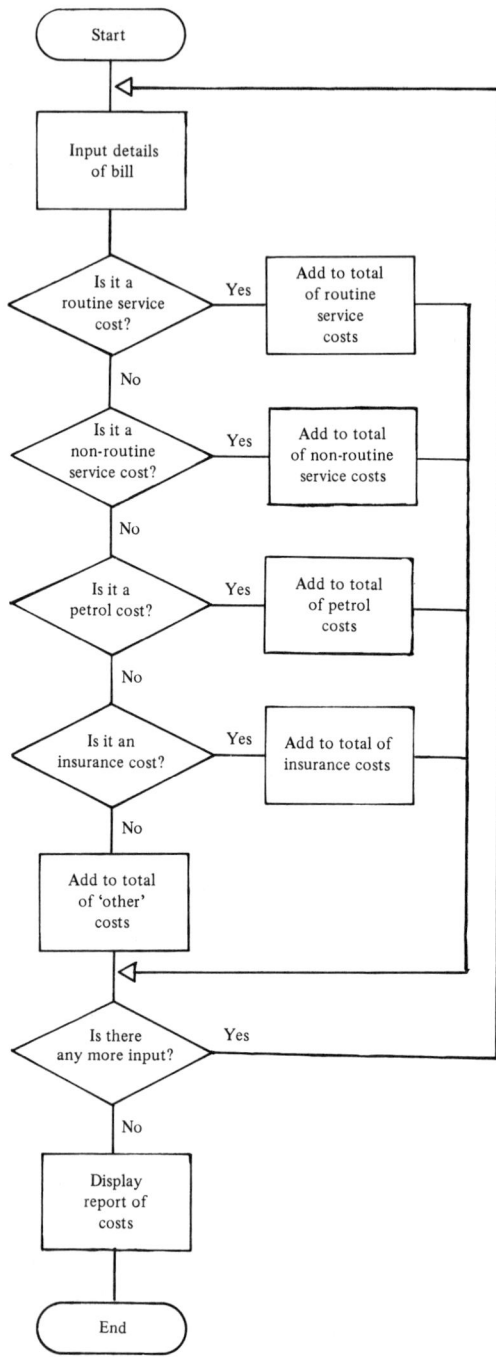

Figure 7.4 Flowcharting as an aid to programming – an example

Although you could keep each step in your head during programming, lots of errors tend to creep in! Remember, you will probably be interrupted occasionally while you are programming and your programs may contain much more complicated options than the example shown. Some people manage very well without flowcharts, but others find the visual presentation of the 'logic' of a program very helpful. I strongly recommend the use of flowcharting for systems design and suggest that you try it out for programming.

DECISION TABLES

The name given to this technique has probably done a great deal to put people off using it! In fact, all that is involved is a very simple tabular way of writing down the various rules that are used within individual information systems to process data. Even if the rules are not written down explicitly at the design stage, as is often the case, the person who writes the programs must have a clear understanding of the rules; decision tables help that process of understanding and also help in the clear recording of ideas and rules.

The best way to see how a decision table works is through an example. Let us take the case of the Christmas card mailing list, described in Chapter 2. The system depends essentially on two ingredients: a list of names and addresses, and a set of rules for deciding whether or not to send a Christmas card. A decision table offers a good way of expressing these rules, as shown in Figure 7.5. Such a decision table is helpful in describing the logic of undertaking certain actions (such as sending a Christmas card) on the basis of certain conditions (such as having received a card the previous year). It also helps clarify your thinking. For example, by looking at Rules 1 and 6, it can be seen that if a card was received from the address for the two previous years then you send a card this year, regardless of whether or not you did so last year. Rule 6 is therefore redundant and we can ignore the last of the three questions if the answers to the first two are positive. Exactly the same applies to Rules 7 and 8. A simplified, consolidated decision table appears therefore as in Figure 7.6.

The same process of analysis could of course be carried out using a flowchart and this is illustrated in Figure 7.7. Many people, however, find the rather complex interconnection of the 'decision boxes' a bit confusing and prefer the more straightforward presentation of a decision table. On the other hand, a flowchart does have the advantage of showing a procedure (that is, the sequence of operations); this can be helpful at the programming stage, where for efficiency's sake you would want to make sure that the first rule tested was the one most likely to be followed. However, the flowchart equivalent is more cumbersome and less easy to change if you want to change one of the rules. The conclusion is therefore not to use either flowcharting or decision tables exclusively,

	Rule 1	Rule 2	Rule 3	Rule 4	Rule 5	Rule 6	Rule 7	Rule 8
Was a card received from this address last year?	Y	Y	N	N	Y	Y	N	N
Was a card received from this address the previous year?	Y	N	Y	Y	N	Y	N	N
Did I send a card to this address last year?	Y	Y	Y	N	N	N	Y	N
Send a card this year	X	X	X			X		
Do not send a card this year				X	X		X	X

Figure 7.5　Decision table for sending Christmas cards

but to use both selectively according to the type of job in hand. An information system or program with lots of procedural steps can be conveniently described with a flowchart; a system — or part of a system — with many combinations of options is relatively simply expressed by means of a decision table. It is quite feasible to use a flowchart for most of the system design and to have one or two decision tables for the more complicated parts.

TESTING METHODS

Testing is an integral part of Step 3 (doing the practical work to turn the idea into the working system). It is not a technique but an activity that requires special attention with regard to method if your information systems are to be effective. The approach and the methods for testing are therefore described here to give you a base for this important part of getting your home computer to do useful work for you.

Firstly, it is worth considering what the main aims are in checking out your freshly created information system. These are:

To make sure everything is working error-free.

To gain full confidence that the system is fulfilling its original goals. This is particularly important if others are going to use your system too.

So it is not simply a matter of seeing if it works; the acceptance and true usefulness of the system also depend on it.

Secondly, although testing itself takes place during Step 3, it should be part of the thinking process at the design stage (during Step 2). Modular design, for example, is a key design concept which leads to major advantages at the testing stage.

Thirdly, plan your testing in a systematic way. Apart from the 'routine' cases (which should of course include the awkward bits, such as year-end totals, leap-year conditions, no data for some months, etc.), assume the worst will happen from time to time. This means, for example:

Testing with completely wrong data (from another system).

Recovering from the situation of switching off your computer in the middle of a run.

Using excessively large volumes of data (too many lines in an address, etc.).

	Rule 1	Rule 2	Rule 3	Rule 4	Rule 5	Rule 6
Was a card received from this address last year?	Y	Y	N	N	Y	N
Was a card received from this address the previous year?	Y	N	Y	Y	N	N
Did I send a card to this address last year?	–	Y	Y	N	N	–
Send a card this year	X	X	X			
Do not send a card this year				X	X	X

Figure 7.6 Simplified decision table for sending Christmas cards

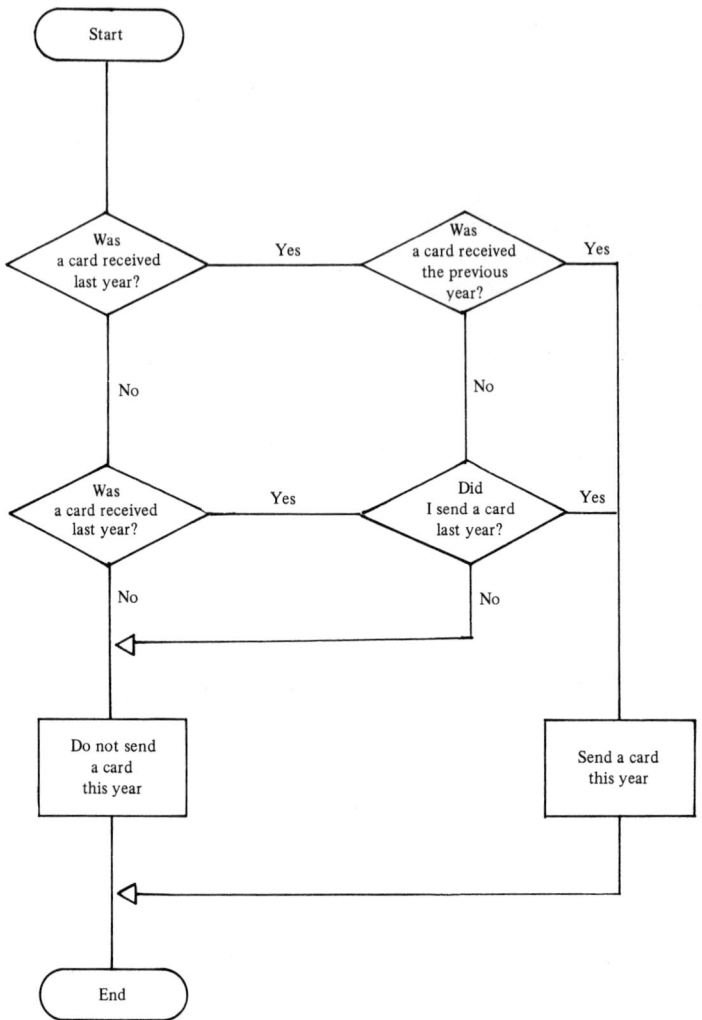

Figure 7.7 Flowchart corresponding to the simplified decision table for sending Christmas cards (shown in Figure 7.6)

Fourthly, undertake the testing itself in a step-by-step fashion. A straightforward approach, applicable to most information systems, is:

Test each program, and, if possible, program module, with your own specially prepared test data.

Test the whole set of programs (if there is more than one program) with your own data, feeding the latter to the first program and letting the system process it through to completion.

Test the entire system in the same way but with 'live' data.

If other persons are going to use the system too, then ask them to provide live data and, if possible, let them have a go at running the system — on the clear understanding that you are still testing (the system will probably go wrong!).

Finally, if you have to make substantial changes to the system to make it work, other than just correcting errors, then be sure to record this carefully. Your working system will not reflect your original design and future changes will be difficult to make if you do not have an accurate description of what is actually going on. This brings us to the subject of documentation.

DOCUMENTATION

Computer specialists are very fond of talking about 'documentation'. This is a rather pompous word for expressing the need to keep a written record of each information system you develop. In the business environment, where personnel responsible for a given system may change, documentation is clearly a key means to ensure continuity. But even in the home-computer environment it is advisable to keep a minimum set of papers which must enable you:

To correct errors in the system.
To build in changes made necessary in the course of time.
To use the system properly and to teach others to do the same (if necessary).
To recreate the system in the event of some unfortunate loss of your files and programs.

These are very important reasons indeed why you should keep some paper record of your work when you develop an information system. In practical terms, it should not mean a lot of work, as it is essentially a matter of assembling in an orderly way papers that you mostly create anyway. So the simplest approach is to use a ring-binder and just insert the collection of papers that you consider necessary to meet the requirements described above. Here is a suggested list of papers you should keep:

1. Your notes on the original idea. A suggested one-page layout is that used to describe the ideas for systems in Chapter 6. Even if you do not create the system immediately after your initial idea, it is useful to collect the summaries for browsing purposes at some future date.

2. The final papers you used to decide on the exact design. These should therefore include: flowcharts, decision tables, file layouts, input descriptions, etc.
3. Programs. If you have a printer, then it is a good idea to list the latest version of each of your programs and put them in the folder with the other papers. If you made changes at a later stage, remember to make a new copy.
4. Instructions for using the system. This includes not only 'how to do it' descriptions, but also notes on security (how often the files are to be copied for storage elsewhere, etc.) and other aspects that are important for keeping the system in good running order.

It may sound as though keeping such a set of papers is a nuisance. It is! But the benefits come later, when you have reached the point of having several different systems on your computer — some working, some in development, some abandoned. When problems arise, when you want to make changes or adapt programs for new purposes, then you will appreciate your collection of key papers!

8   The Pitfalls and the Fun

The main purpose of this book has been to make the reader aware that having a
home computer is not only fun but *useful*. There is little more satisfying than
making that machine work for you. As this book has attempted to show, this
can be achieved in a variety of ways, using a systematic approach. But of course
nothing is as simple as it sounds.

This chapter is therefore aimed at encouraging the reader to try his or her
skills in further, more adventurous ways, but at the same time drawing attention to the various traps into which the unwary could fall.

Let us first look at some of the pitfalls to be avoided. Here are some 'golden
rules'.

1. Don't bury your home computer in the cellar!
Your computer must be easily accessible if it is to be used as part of the daily
life in your home. Nothing deters use more than if you have to go up or down
steps, open a cupboard, lift one or several devices out, clear a working surface
and connect up cables, just to be able to start using the machine.

Ideally, your machine should be situated very conveniently near your normal
household operations and be ready to use almost at the flick of a switch. Furniture is now available that can house your home computer and all its attachments
(including cassette tapes, etc.) in one handy unit. The nearer one is to this ideal
of convenient access, the better are the chances of exploiting your home computer to the full.

2. Remember – computers only impress if they work!
In Chapter 5, the KISS (Keep It Simple, Stupid!) approach was discussed,
emphasising that attempts to be clever in information systems tend to result
in errors and difficult-to-use systems. This design philosophy can be taken a
step further, namely: a *good* system is one that *works*!

It is always sound to aim for efficiency, but in the last resort the one question that has to be answered positively for the work to mean anything at all is:
Does it work?

The essential lesson to be drawn from this is that the objectives at all times
must be to ensure that the system runs error-free. The user should not have to
worry about 'certain conditions' that cause problems. It can be irritating to
wait seconds or even minutes while a computer system performs some task, but
it is *infuriating* if a hiccup occurs, so making the whole process a waste of time.
So remember: reliability first, efficiency second.

3. Make your systems 'user friendly'

The term 'user friendly' is one frequently quoted nowadays. Although the term itself is rather inelegant, the idea behind it is very sensible indeed. It is intended to point out the need to focus the design of the system on ease and convenience of use. Many ingenious information systems have met their downfall because the user found them difficult or awkward to use. The moral therefore is to make each of your information systems as easy to use as possible. But bear in mind that simplicity alone is not enough. 'User friendliness' includes the important idea of convenience, too. Nobody likes having to start the same procedure all over again if they have made a minor error.

A particularly frequent problem is to allow for both experienced and inexperienced users. The latter need a lot of help with very explicit instructions on what to do next, especially when things go wrong. On the other hand the experienced user finds it annoying to be given elaborate instructions every time a small slip occurs. One solution is to let the user specify right at the start if he or she is experienced or not, so that the system can offer alternative levels of support for the two broad types of user. Even then, though, it is good design practice to allow the experienced user, too, to call in as much help as required.

4. Don't keep improving the system!

That may sound a curious piece of advice, but at some stage you must decide either that the system is now good enough (with all its imperfections) or that it must be abandoned. The development phase of a new information system *must* have a definite end. Emergency corrections of 'bugs' in the system have of course to be put right, just as modifications to take care of outside factors (such as a change in the method of mortgage payments) must be made. But the temptation should be resisted to fiddle with a working system to gain marginal improvements.

Changes tend to introduce errors and, even if they do work perfectly, it is a nuisance for the user to have to become familiar with constant 'improvements'. So — best leave well alone!

5. Remember — others will view your systems differently

There is a natural pride in achieving a working information system. But beware that even if it meets (in your opinion) its objectives, others may be less impressed. If these other persons are onlookers, then perhaps this does not matter too much; the view of other users of your system, however, is all-important. Understanding the reasons for their lack of enthusiasm is paramount. You may well find that the system is too complicated or unreliable or it may be a problem of learning to use the system properly or of locating the computer in the right place.

If such problems can be overcome — fine. But, if they are not overcome, then you should accept the sensible course of scrapping the system completely. The effort will have been worthwhile in the long term, because of the experience gained. The main point to remember is that the value of the system is dependent on what all the users think of it, not just what you, rightly or wrongly, feel.

The above points are useful ones to remember as potential pitfalls. It would be a pity, however, to end this book on a warning note, as the pleasures and possibilities far outweigh the dangers. The remainder of this chapter is therefore devoted to opening up wider horizons, by pointing towards some ambitious ways of using your home computer.

INTEGRATED SYSTEMS

The uncomplicated approach has been stressed throughout this book. The chances of success are directly related to the simplicity of the design. Among the ways this simplicity can be maintained is to make each information system you develop a 'stand-alone' system, (that is, it does not depend on any other system for input). As a general policy for achieving working systems, this is always valid. But at some stage you will inevitably reach the situation where you will wonder why you have two files of addresses or two sets of accounts on household expenditures. You will see that savings in time and effort in updating, etc., could be obtained if two of your information systems shared a common file or produced one report for two purposes, instead of two separate ones.

This appreciation of sharing data and programs is a natural phase in systems development and clearly has much merit. It does mean, though, that you will have to be very careful about introducing a change into any of your systems if one or more other systems depend on some part of it.

In other words, there are real benefits in integrating your various information systems — but there are very real dangers, too. In the home-computer environment, it is best to follow a very cautious policy towards systems integration. Integration of systems makes it much more difficult to isolate errors and problem areas.

So my advice is: by all means let your information systems evolve slowly towards some integration. That is part of the fun of home-computing. But — and it is a big 'but' — bear in mind the value of the KISS (Keep It Simple, Stupid!) approach and proceed step by step. Rushing into systems integration invariably leads to major problems.

DATA BASE APPROACH

The sharing of files was mentioned above as one aspect of systems integration. When this aspect becomes highly developed, one starts to talk about 'data bases'. These are collections of data organised in a sufficiently flexible way to allow

them to serve as sources of information for several different information systems.
A simple example might be that you keep all addresses (Christmas card list,
general addresses, insurance companies, magazine publishers, etc.) on a single
file, which is then used in conjunction with other files and programs particular
to a given information purpose (for example, insurance payments or ordering
books). Your updating programs and the general procedures for handling the
'address data base' would, however, be common to all these information systems.

Advantages of the data base approach are avoidance of duplication of data
and the economies in setting up quite sophisticated 'find-and-display' methods,
such as those described in Chapter 5. As in the case of integrated systems, the
disadvantage is increased complexity and the more wide-reaching effects of
errors. However, one of the encouraging trends in the home-computer market
is the increasing availability of off-the-shelf programs for running such home
data bases. You still need to do a lot of work to organise your data appropriately
but the difficult programming job is done for you.

ACCESS TO OUTSIDE SERVICES

You will be under constant temptation to increase the power of your home
computer. You will hear about programs that seem to be just what you want —
but need more central memory than your machine or require more disc storage.
You will also hear about large data bases, which have just the information you
need. These things will bring home sadly the fact that however much you invest
in your home computer it can never match the tremendous range of facilities
available in the 'outside world'. At some stage therefore, after you have success-
fully used your computer in your own home, it is worth looking at the possibilities
for effectively extending its power enormously by accessing outside, commercial
services. These fall broadly into three kinds:

> Processing power. This type of service simply places at your disposal the
> power of a large (at least compared to your own) computer. So you link
> up to it in order to run programs that would not 'fit' on to your own com-
> puter or that would take too long to run. You pay on an 'as-used' basis.
> Software. The preceding facility — processing power — is rarely offered
> alone; the service organisation providing the computer almost always has a
> wide range of programs (software) that can help you (for example, languages
> more powerful than BASIC) and that you can also use directly. These are
> charged for, naturally. Some of these ready-to-use programs will be of general
> use, such as one for calculating statistical parameters for a given set of num-
> bers, whereas others will be more tailored to specific groups, such as account-
> ing routines.

Data bases. There are well over a thousand data bases publicly available almost worldwide on a wide range of subjects, including such varying topics as medicine, building, stocks and shares, sports, etc. The usual charges are based on the data you find that meets your need and for the computer time you have used.

These are all obviously very powerful ways of extending the usefulness of your own computer. Now for the disadvantages! These are twofold:

Technical connection. To use any of the above facilities, you need to become a customer of (1) the supplier of the computer service and (2) the telecommunications supplier, that is, the organisation that will enable you to dial up the service (in the U.S.A., this would be a common carrier or a value-added network operator such as Tymnet or Telenet; in the United Kingdom, it would be British Telecom, etc.). Both will issue you with account numbers and passwords, for charging and for privacy purposes. They will advise you on the technical requirements for connection, but you will need to fulfil these yourself. This implies buying or renting an interface device (a 'modem') and making your computer operate in telecommunications mode according to the standards laid down. At the present time these are normally 'teletype' standards or packet-switching (X25) standards recommended by the international organisation CCITT (International Telegraph and Telephone Consultative Committee). You have to be very experienced to implement these on your home computer, but fortunately the suppliers of home computers are more and more recognising the usefulness of being able to use these machines not only as stand-alone devices at home but also as 'intelligent terminals' which can link to other and bigger machines. One can expect therefore that the necessary standards will more and more become part of the normal home computer, opening up the possibilities mentioned above. There will still be plenty of work left for you, however! You can program your home computer to do the dialling and make the connection to whatever other service you want to use with the minimum of fuss.
Costs. Unless you are rich or have a substantial need for using outside services, you are likely to use them very sparingly. The reason is simply that of cost. In real terms, the prices charged are very modest and many businesses use outside services heavily. For the home user, the amounts may seem relatively high. To dial and use a large data base typically costs a bit more than one dollar a minute. A normal 'search' on a data base lasts around 10 minutes, so you can reckon on paying 12–15 dollars every time you look for a piece of information. In terms of value for money, this is still very, very good, but obviously you cannot afford to let the family loose on all the data bases they fancy!

So, in summary, then, the use of outside services offers an explosion in possibilities for using your home computer, but there are technical problems to be solved, beyond the complete beginner, and cost aspects that have to be taken very seriously.

ON-LINE CONTROL SYSTEMS

The information systems described in this book have all been of the kind where human intervention (for example, entering data on the keyboard) is an integral part of the functioning of the system. This last section is meant to draw your attention to a further sphere of potential use for your home computer, namely letting it monitor and control some activity directly, without your own participation — beyond of course developing the system in the first place and switching it on and off.

Examples of this kind of use are:

Security systems. Here you use your computer to monitor a number of sensors placed near windows, doors, hallways, etc., and to take some action (such as sounding an alarm) when one of the devices is triggered. This can be used for detecting intruders or for smoke detectors.

Heating-control system. A very beneficial way of using a home computer is to let it control the way heat is distributed throughout your home. By feeding it with information from sensors in each room, the central heating unit and from one outside (to measure the external temperature), you can ensure optimum heat generation. Some central heating systems come with their own microprocessors which do this too, but in my experience none of them yet match the performance achieved by home-programmed systems.

Model railway control. Quite sophisticated control of points, signals, crossings, etc., on model railway systems can be achieved through a home computer. As the system grows, the logic required to control the system can become very complex indeed.

The type of use of your home computer described above requires more than the ability to design an information system. You also need to be able to wire up sensors (temperature measurers, pressure detectors, photocell units, etc.) and connect them to your computer. This is beyond the scope of this book, but there is plenty of guidance available through suppliers of such devices and through magazines on personal computing. If you do see a good potential application for your home computer in this field, then it is well worth pursuing as it is usually a very rewarding effort — in both financial and personal satisfaction terms. Bear in mind, though, that this type of application often requires dedicated use of your computer (such as the heating-control system). So you will probably need a second machine for your other information systems.

Hopefully, the above sections have suggested to you some new avenues for exploring potential uses for your home-computer system. As indicated, there are some major pitfalls, but most of them — though not all — can be avoided. In the process, you can anyway be sure that you will have fun too!

Index

Accounting applications 51
Address book 3, 9, 56
Amendments 32–4, 36, 64–5, 67,
   73–4, 76
Animal breeding 58
Antique collecting 45

Back-up 15, 27, 41
BASIC 1, 3, 78
Batch updating 32–4
Benefits 12, 15, 21
Billiard scores 47
Binary searching 38–9
Bird watching 45

Camping checklist 59
Car maintenance 16–21, 22
Cassettes 30–33, 36, 40
CCITT (International Telegraph and
   Telephone Consultative Committee)
   79
Checklists 59
Christmas card list 4–9, 69, 70, 71, 72
Coding 18–20
Configuration 30
Costs 12, 36, 79

Darts scores 47
Data bases 29, 77–8, 79
Data collection 5, 14, 18, 24
Data definition 17–18
Data handling 28–36
Data management systems 29, 36
Decision tables 69–70, 71
Design 1, 6–7, 11, 12–14, 19, 26–41
Diary 53
Dictionary 36
Diet plan and weight record 43
Discettes 30
Discs 30, 31, 32, 36, 40
Display 37–40
Documentation 14, 73–4

Electronic diary 15, 53
Electronic notebook 44
Examination question spotting 50

Family medical history 62
Family tree 58
Feasibility study 1, 16
File handling 28–36
File organisation 19–20, 30–36
File searching 38–40
File sharing 77
File structure 13–14, 19, 30–36
Files 5, 7, 14, 16, 24, 28, 77–8
Find and display 37–40
Flowcharting 33, 64–9
Football pools forecasting 49
Football scores 47
Format (output) 37–8
Furniture 75

Games 1, 3
Golf scores 37, 47

Heating-control systems 80
Heating-cost monitoring 55
Hobby index 45–8
Holiday planning 59
Homework schedule 52
Hotel and restaurant list 61
House-building control 60
Human aspects 8, 76

Implementation problems 20, 27
Index files (*see also* File organisation)
   38
Input 6, 11, 13, 14, 29
Input validation 29–30, 40–41
Insurance 41
Insurance system 54
Integrated systems 77

Interactive computing 29
Inventory systems 48

Keys 22, 33
KISS approach 27, 75, 77
Knitting index 45

Languages (foreign), teach yourself
    systems 63
Languages (programming) 3, 78
Languages (search) 39–40
List structures 36, 38
Log-book 10

Magazine subscriptions 21, 23–5
Medical history 62
Memory size 11, 36, 78
Menus 44
Merging 33–6
Model railway control 80
Modem 79
Modifications 14, 28, 73–4, 76
Modular design 28, 30, 41, 72
Mortgage payments 51

Notebook (electronic) 44, 59

On-line control systems 80
Output 6, 13, 18, 24, 37–8
Overflow 36

Packet-switching 79
Pointers 36
Printout 11, 59
Processing 6, 13
Programming 1, 3, 28, 38–9, 64–5,
    68, 69–70
Program(s) 5, 7, 8, 14, 20, 24, 29, 32,
    34, 35, 38, 72–3, 74

RAM 30
Random files 36
Reading list 44
Reasonableness checks 30
Recipes and menus 44
Record 31–3, 38, 39, 41
Recovery 41
Reliability 27, 40–41, 75
Restaurant list 61
Retrieval 36, 37–40
ROM 30
Routines 3, 30

Search language 39–40
Searching 38–40
Security 20, 40–41
Security systems 80
Sequential files 30, 32–6, 38–9
Software 3, 36, 78
Sorting 33–6, 67
Sports scores 47
Stamp collecting 45
System specification 12
Systems analysis and design 1,
    3–4, 10–15, 26–41
Systems analysts 3
Systems development 1

Teach yourself systems 63
Telecommunications 79
Teletype 79
Testing 7, 8, 14, 20, 24, 70–73
Transport timetable 57

Updating 28, 32–4, 64–7
User friendliness 39, 76
User(s) 12, 26–7, 39, 76

Wedding present list 59
Wine list 48

X25 79

SHROPSHIRE LIBRARIES

Please return or renew before the last date stamped below. Renewal may
be in person or by telephone, providing it is not required by another user.
Please quote details on label below.
LS.105